Spiced RIGHT

Flavorful cooking with *herbs* **and** *spices*

To Debbie,
from one
passionate
cook to
another!

Sandra Bowens

Sandra Bowens

This is for Tom. Mahalo for giving me the time to finish my masterpiece and for all of your tasteful suggestions.

Contents

Acknowledgements

Thanks to…

…Tom for always being an enthusiastic participant in recipe development and tasting as well as pushing me along when I needed it.

…Mom and Dad for allowing me the childhood freedom to develop a passion and for all your encouragement over the years.

…Virginia, Tom, Sergei, Isaac, Landon and Layla for always being willing to try something new in my kitchen or theirs.

…Mark and Carol and Terry for always acting as if I were doing them the favor when they were actually helping me out.

…Russ and Janice for always being ready to sample my latest experiment.

…Linda B. and Luanne and Alan for always giving me constructive feedback and encouragement.

…all my Whatcom County Master Gardener and Semiahmoo Yacht Club friends who knowingly or unwittingly taste-tested my creations.

…Linda T. for showing me just how many times I use the word "just" as she waded through my pages as an editor.

…the many readers of my website over the years who wrote in with questions I couldn't answer—forcing me to learn new things or develop new recipes.

Introduction

As the world becomes a smaller place, our spice cabinets grow deeper. Mysterious flavors we once thought of as ancient history, galangal and sumac, cubeb and grains of paradise, are showing up at markets and even the local grocery store. Fenugreek and cinnamon are considered health food while tidy packages of fresh herbs earn more and more space in the produce department of the local supermarket.

But why buy fresh herbs when you can experience the pleasure of growing your own? The smallest of places can accommodate a few pots of choice herbs. Herb plants are attractive enough to tuck into more traditional landscaping, or worthy of a little garden all their own. Just make sure it's close to the kitchen.

Spices are another matter. Who among us can tend a 50-foot allspice tree that requires year-round sunshine and ample amounts of rainfall? How many saffron crocuses are you willing to plant given that it takes 70,000 flowers to amass a pound of threads? I would be happy to grow paprika peppers if only I could learn the secrets of success that the Spaniards and Hungarians know.

We must not despair at our own limitations. Purveyors of fine spices abound. Look for companies that specialize and offer their goods in an assortment of quantities. For freshness sake, it is best to order frequently rather than stockpile supplies. As often as possible buy whole spices that you can grind yourself as you need them. An electric coffee grinder makes this a snap. Just keep it far away from the coffee beans to avoid nasty surprises like chile powder in your morning brew.

I've been learning about herbs and spices for half of my life now. The love affair began nearly 25 years ago. I landed a job selling Colorado Spice Company seasonings to restaurants. To a cook, it was a magical job, one that allowed me entrance to kitchens throughout Denver, privy to the spicy secrets of how different chefs flavored their specialties.

A whole new world blossomed for me as I began to write a training manual for the company. I delved into how different seasonings had been used in the past, where they come from and how they are processed. It is an exotic business, the spice trade. Goods are plucked from trees in places like Indonesia or Madagascar. Farmers must protect their crops fiercely, sometimes even sleeping with them to prevent theft, as is the case with vanilla beans as they cure.

Prior to the Colorado Spice Company job, I had always worked in the front of the house at restaurants. Starting as a busgirl way back when, I went into management once of age. The sojourn with the spices gave me the impetus to pursue positions in the back of the house as a cook. You know how a life goes sometimes. My husband's work kept us on the move so I often found myself casting about for a new job. I found that I really liked working on my own.

I did stints as the cook at a 60-man fraternity house, a 9-girl foster home, even as a camp cook on several occasions. I presented cooking classes and demonstrations. It is fun to tell people that I once demonstrated making deep-fried ice cream sundaes for 110 people—and they all had one. Never again!

Eventually I found my way back to dining establishments, and prepared wood-fired pizzas at a place so popular we turned a profit from day one. I rose early to bake biscuits and muffins and make chocolate mousse for a boutique hotel. At one bakery near New Orleans I handmade thousands of mini-pastries each weekend and learned how to design entire villages from gingerbread.

At different intervals, I had the opportunity to travel. Italy opened my eyes to real Italian cooking. Korea taught me more about seafood than I thought there was to know. The markets in Singapore held spices of which I had only heard. Hungary told me the real story about paprika. Germany, Nicaragua, Mexico, everywhere I have been has been an eye-opening culinary education.

Food took on new meaning when we moved to Mongolia where boiled mutton is the national dish. Cooking and eating became a great adventure. The central market consisted of rows of stalls filled with mostly unfamiliar foods and our apartment's kitchen housed miniature appliances. I persevered, however, and soon we had Friday night pizza parties, unusual omelets and yummy versions of tuna salads.

All along, on the side I continued an ongoing study of herbs and spices. My debut writing about them was a column for the Reno-Gazette Journal. Years later that series of articles formed the foundation of my website, aPinchOf.com.

Now I offer you this book. It is filled with recipes that never found a home on the website and some that did but are too good to exclude.

Happy cooking!

A Few Notes on Ingredients

As you make your way through these pages you may find a few ingredients that are unfamiliar to you. I won't go through individual herbs and spices here, you can find that information at the website www.aPinchOf.com, but perhaps I should explain some of my favorite pantry items.

Whole wheat pastry flour: This is a finely milled whole wheat flour. It adds fiber and nutrition to baked goods without that heavy texture. I also find that baked goods don't dry out as quickly when using pastry flour instead of traditional whole wheat flour. Look for whole wheat pastry flour in the natural foods section of your supermarket or order it online.

Pickled jalapenos: I always have a jar of sliced and pickled jalapenos in the refrigerator, with a backup jar in the pantry. You'll see them in many different recipes here. You can find them on the pickle aisle or with the other Mexican foods at the supermarket.

Chipotle paste: Chipotles are smoked jalapenos packed in a spicy adobo sauce. They are smoking hot but so delicious. If you can't find a prepared paste, consider whirling a whole can in the food processor. Store the paste in a glass container in the refrigerator. You will find small cans of chipotles in adobo sauce for sale with other Mexican ingredients.

Oils: These recipes call for a wide variety of oils. You will see olive, extra virgin olive, sesame, walnut and peanut. When a recipe calls for vegetable oil, I will most often use a product called Saffola because it seems the healthiest to me. You could use canola or whatever you like, of course.

Turbinado sugar: Also known as Sugar-in-the-Raw, I like using this less processed version of sugar in certain cases. It can add a nice crunch to some dishes. You'll find it with the other sugars in the supermarket or you can get it at a health food store.

Milk: All of the recipes that call for milk have been tested with either whole or 2 percent milk, most often the latter.

Buttermilk powder: Fluid buttermilk will make baked goods more tender. Sometimes you want that effect without all the liquid, that's where the powder comes in. It is also handy to keep on the shelf in case you don't have any buttermilk in the refrigerator.

If you are a fan of cilantro or mushrooms, you may note their absence on these pages. Sadly, I am in the percentage of the population that finds cilantro tastes like soap. With a few classic exceptions, I avoid it as much as possible. I'm guessing that if you like it, you will find the places where you could toss in a handful with good results.

I wish I liked mushrooms. I really do. Over the years I have tried every new mushroom I can, tasted them in different preparations and keep hoping that they won't taste like dirt to me. No luck. We must all cook to satisfy ourselves first, so you won't find any 'shrooms in these pages. Again, I'm certain that if you like mushrooms you will see where they might fit into a recipe and can add enough to make yourself happy.

Onion Tarts, page 21

Appetizers and Snacks: The fun foods

Appetizers and snacks are the fun foods.

This is where all of your efforts at tending an herb garden will be rewarded. The simplest garden of basil, thyme, chives, dill, cilantro and arugula provides a wealth of inspiration. When it comes to deciding if you want to make Nutty Cheese Puffs or Onion Tarts, check the garden to see whether you have arugula or thyme in greater abundance. Fresh chile peppers and a handful of cilantro will put you on the fast track to Quick Fresh Salsa.

Combining herbs is always a learning experience. As long as it's fresh, just about anything goes for the Herbed Ricotta Spread, but you are bound to discover that tarragon has a tendency to dominate or that chervil may go unnoticed if companion herbs are in too great a number.

You also may notice that fresh herbs provide a dramatically different flavor than their dried counterparts. I never cared much for tarragon or rosemary until I began to grow them. Their distinct fresh taste just doesn't translate through the dried leaf.

Oregano is a different matter. It is one of the few herbs that most people prefer in the dried form. The fresh leaves are somewhat astringent while the dried leaves are strong yet subtle. However, oregano is an attractive plant in the herb garden. It has a mounding form that must be reigned in or it will spread like mad, but that is easy enough to deal with by snipping back those running roots.

The preparation of appetizers takes you into experimental territory. Chiles and all the different peppers can make for fascinating exploration. The chiles used in this chapter's recipes range from the tame canned green chile to the fiery cayenne.

Quick Fresh Salsa provides an excellent foundation for testing out the wide variety of fresh chiles you may come across in the marketplace. Start with Anaheim chiles for a mild salsa. Intensify the heat with a jalapeno or go bold with the sturdy and often powerful poblano.

Roasting these same chile peppers mellows their flavors, or in the case of the chipotle, creates a whole new sensation. Chipotles are smoked jalapenos with the potential to make your ears smolder. For ease in handling, I like to use a paste that's available in small jars. In most cases, half a teaspoon or so will go a long way. Roasted red peppers and pickled jalapenos are wonderful kitchen staples. Keep canned diced green chiles on hand to liven up foods like quesadillas or even eggs at a moment's notice. Tabasco sauce or the equivalent is sometimes just the little kick a dish needs.

You will see dried chiles and assorted peppers come up again and again throughout these recipes. Basic black pepper takes on different nuances depending on how it is ground. A finely ground black pepper winds its way through a dish whereas coarsely ground peppercorns offer a spicy bite just where you put it. Cayenne brings a bright, hot taste that is an interesting alternative to the dusky undertones of black pepper.

Dried chiles can be purchased whole or ground, adding yet another dimension to the well-seasoned realm. These are not at all the blend of spices you find in a supermarket labeled as "chili powder." They are single peppers that, like fresh chiles, range from mild to intense.

All paprikas are not created equal, either. Your basic California paprika may offer some taste along with a nice splash of color, but to really elevate flavors, investigate the imported varieties. Spanish paprikas range from smoky to the savory side of sweet, while Hungarian types can go from mildly fruity to hot, hot, hot. If you would like to conduct a taste test, make the Three Layer Cheese Ball, but on the layer with the paprika mixed in, try it two ways: Hungarian on one half and Spanish on the other.

Epazote is an herb that may be unfamiliar. This Mexican native is most often associated with beans, but it is equally at home in the Quesadillas with Zucchini-Epazote Filling. Epazote is a tough-leaved herb that is better cooked into a dish than used fresh and raw at the last minute. You may have to search a bit to find it available dried, so consider growing a plant in your garden.

Don't overlook using food preparation as part of the entertainment at your next friendly get-together. Appetizers like the Toasted Ravioli or the Restaurant Nachos are best eaten right away so why not get your guests involved?

While savory appetizers and snacks are the norm, occasionally the Festive Fruit Platter with Poppy Seed Dip is just right. Freshly cut fruits are a welcome addition to a buffet or a healthy alternative to other more calorie-laden treats. By serving the black and white dip surrounded with colorful fruit, the ordinary becomes an extra special centerpiece.

The majority of these recipes can be made ahead so that you have time to enjoy the party. By keeping a few choice ingredients on hand, you will also be able to whip up a tasty tidbit at a moment's notice.

SAVORY ASIDE

What's a Scoville Heat Unit?

Wilbur Scoville developed his test for measuring the heat found in hot peppers in 1912.

Heat units are determined by how many parts of sugar water it takes to dilute a sample so that the heat of a chile can no longer be detected. The chile sample is provided in the form of an extract. Mr. Scoville's test has become the industry standard for determining just how hot "hot" really is.

Today, you will often find the Scoville Heat Unit rating on a jar of salsa or a bottle of hot sauce.

A jalapeno falls in at roughly 4000 heat units while the habanero rates an easy 250,000. Generally accepted levels are as follows: 0-5000—Mild; 5000-20,000—Medium; 20,000-70,000—Hot; and 70,000-300,000—Extreme.

Spicy Nut Mix

Here is a flavorful snack that's a snap to prepare and keeps well. For this, use a prepared chili powder blend rather than a single chile pepper.

---

    2 cups (about 12 ounces) mixed nuts
    4 teaspoons vegetable oil
    4 teaspoons chili powder

Preheat the oven to 350 degrees. Place the nuts on a baking sheet and toast in the oven for 10 minutes. Remove; transfer to a small bowl. Drizzle with the oil and sprinkle with the chili powder. Toss the nuts to coat; return to the oven for 3 minutes more. Cool and store in an airtight container.

Makes 2 cups

Savory White Bean Puree with toasted pita chips

Tasty pita chips are available in the supermarket snack aisle these days, so you may choose to skip the step of preparing your own. If you do decide to make them yourself, enhance the chips even further by mixing up your own onion salt (1 part salt to 2 parts granulated onion). This silky puree is a good illustration of how to punch up the flavor of dried herbs; we chop fresh parsley leaves with the dried savory for an extra flavor step.

---

    4 pita breads
    2 Tablespoons olive oil, divided
    $\frac{1}{2}$ teaspoon onion salt
    $\frac{1}{2}$ cup minced yellow onion
    1 Tablespoon fresh flat-leaf parsley leaves
    1 teaspoon dried savory

1 clove garlic, minced
¼ teaspoon dried thyme
Pinches of cayenne
Pinches of freshly milled black pepper
1 can (15 ounces) white beans, rinsed and drained
¼ cup (approximately) beef stock (or use chicken or vegetable stock)
2 teaspoons extra-virgin olive oil
½ cup diced tomato
1 small jalapeno pepper, stemmed, seeded and minced

Preheat the oven to 350 degrees.

Cut the pita breads into six triangles and split each into two pieces by carefully tearing the edges apart. Arrange in a single layer on a baking sheet. Brush lightly on both sides with 1 Tablespoon of the olive oil and sprinkle with the onion salt. Bake for about 12 minutes or until light brown and crisp.

Heat the remaining 1 Tablespoon of the olive oil in a small saucepan over medium-high heat. Add the onion; cook, stirring often, for 3 minutes. Meanwhile, chop the fresh parsley leaves with the dried savory and add to the saucepan along with the garlic and thyme and a few pinches each of cayenne and black pepper. Cook and stir a few more minutes until the onion begins to brown. Add the beans and ¼ cup stock; cook and stir to heat through.

Using a hand-held blender (or a potato masher) puree the beans, adding more stock if needed, to make a smooth paste. Taste for seasonings. Stir in the 2 teaspoons of extra-virgin olive oil and a bit more cayenne, if desired. Transfer to a serving bowl and garnish around the edges with a circle of the diced tomato sprinkled with the minced jalapeno. Arrange the pita chips around the bowl. Serve warm or at room temperature.

Makes about 2 cups

Seeded Hummus

Most hummus recipes call for tahini, but you may not have that on hand. This version uses sesame seeds instead. Toast the seeds by shaking them in a small dry skillet over medium-high heat until their color deepens and they become fragrant. As a dip, hummus is divine, but it makes a delicious sandwich spread as well. Garlic makes its presence known here; if you aren't a big fan, cut back to two cloves.

---

2 Tablespoons white sesame seeds, toasted
4 cloves garlic, peeled and quartered
2 Tablespoons olive oil
1 can (15 ounces) garbanzo beans, rinsed and drained
3 Tablespoons fresh lemon juice
2 Tablespoons plain yogurt, plus 2 teaspoons for garnish
$\frac{1}{2}$ teaspoon ground cumin, plus more for garnish
$\frac{1}{2}$ teaspoon salt
$\frac{1}{4}$ teaspoon cayenne, or to taste, plus more for garnish
Assorted fresh cut vegetables
Toasted pita bread cut into triangles

In the bowl of a food processor fitted with the steel blade, place the sesame seeds, garlic and olive oil. Process briefly, until the garlic is chopped fine.

Add the garbanzo beans, lemon juice, yogurt, cumin, salt and cayenne; process until smooth. Taste and adjust seasonings, if necessary.

To serve, place the hummus in a shallow dish; top with a dollop of yogurt in the center and sprinkle with cumin and cayenne. Arrange the vegetables and pita triangles around the dish.

Hummus will keep covered in the refrigerator for about five days. Allow it to come to room temperature before serving.

Makes 1½ cups

Almond-Red Pepper Dip

I came up with this yummy dip for a holiday get-together where the host requested we bring appetizers to share. The bright orangey-red color seemed to get as much attention as the deep, rich flavor. These are ingredients you can keep in the pantry so you can whip it up when the whim strikes. Other herbs like thyme or dried oregano, even just parsley, would work well, too. Marjoram was one of the few fresh herbs I had in the garden in December.

---

1 cup slivered almonds
1 jar (10 ounces) roasted piquillo peppers, drained
2 small cloves garlic, peeled and quartered
2 Tablespoons extra-virgin olive oil
1 Tablespoon sherry vinegar
2 teaspoons minced fresh marjoram
1/4 teaspoon salt, or to taste
4 turns of the peppermill, or to taste
Pita chips
Assorted fresh cut vegetables

Toast the almonds by shaking them in a dry skillet over medium-high heat until they are slightly browned and aromatic. Allow to cool on a plate before using.

Place the cooled almonds along with the remaining ingredients (roasted peppers through black pepper) into the bowl of a food processor fitted with the steel blade. Process to a smooth paste. Taste and adjust seasonings as necessary.

Serve at room temperature with pita chips and/or fresh vegetables for dipping.

Makes about 1 1/2 cups

Chipotle-Jack Dip

I was flattered into developing this recipe when, after eating something similar from the supermarket deli, my husband said, "You could make this and it would be even better." You will want to have plenty of chips on hand for dipping, this stuff is addictive! If you buy the chipotles in a can be sure to transfer them into a glass jar (they will stain plastic) before storing in the refrigerator.

---

2 small green onions, sliced (both whites and greens) about 3 Tablespoons
¾ cup sour cream
¼ cup mayonnaise
¾ teaspoon adobo sauce from canned chipotles (or use chipotle paste)
¼ teaspoon ground cumin
¼ teaspoon salt
1½ cups (4 ounces) shredded pepper-jack cheese

In a medium bowl, mix together the green onions, sour cream, mayonnaise, adobo sauce, cumin and salt. Stir in the shredded cheese. Allow to sit for about 15 minutes to develop flavors. Taste for seasonings; adjust as necessary. Serve with potato chips or fresh veggies.

Makes 1½ cups

Quick Fresh Salsa

You will find yourself using this for more than just dipping chips. Try it on eggs, mix it with chopped avocado for a refreshing salad or use it to garnish cooked corn kernels. Roasting the onion, jalapeno, tomatoes and garlic takes extra time but gives a more intense flavor. Simply run the ingredients under a broiler until deeply brown, blackened really, on all sides before proceeding with the recipe.

---

1 medium yellow onion, quartered
1 fresh jalapeno, stemmed and quartered (seeded, if desired)
3 medium tomatoes, cored and seeded
1 clove garlic, roughly chopped
2 teaspoons lime juice
1 Tablespoon packed fresh cilantro leaves
¾ teaspoon kosher salt

In a food processor fitted with the steel blade, coarsely chop the onion. Add the remaining ingredients and use the pulse action until the tomatoes are chopped fine. (Alternatively, you can finely chop the vegetables by hand.) Taste for seasonings; adjust if necessary.

Serve right away or store in refrigerator up to three days.

Makes about 2½ cups

Restaurant Nachos

This method is so much better than a pile of chips on a plate. Tostada shells are flat, crisp-fried corn tortillas. Look for them alongside other Mexican ingredients at the supermarket. Broiling to melt the cheese really does go fast so, as the recipe suggests, be sure to prepare your serving dishes before popping the nachos into the oven. Cooked ground beef, taco filling, steak strips or shredded chicken are welcome additions to this basic recipe. Use them in place of the refried beans or layer onto the nachos between the beans and cheese.

---

3 tostada shells
³/₄ cup refried beans, warmed
³/₄ cup (about 2 ounces) finely grated cheddar cheese
12 slices jarred pickled jalapeno
¹/₂ cup shredded lettuce
¹/₄ cup prepared guacamole, or use Poblano-Avocado Topping (page 19)
¹/₄ cup sour cream
¹/₄ cup Quick Fresh Salsa (page 9), or use jarred salsa

Arrange an oven rack about 6 inches under the broiler unit and preheat.

Spread the tostada shells evenly with the refried beans and place on a baking sheet. Sprinkle the cheese evenly over the beans. Place 4 jalapeno slices, at 12, 3, 6 and 9 as if on a clock, on each of the prepared tostada shells. Set aside while you prepare the serving dish.

In the center of a serving platter, make a flat pile with the shredded lettuce. Top this with dollops of the guacamole, sour cream and salsa.

Place the baking sheet under the broiler and allow the cheese to melt and become bubbly. Watch carefully, this will only take minutes. Remove from broiler and cut into quarters using a large knife or pizza wheel.

Arrange these nacho quarters in a ring around the prepared garnishes and serve immediately.

Makes 12 pieces

Quesadilla with Zucchini-Epazote Filling

If you can't find epazote, use Mexican oregano or marjoram. Nearly any sort of melting cheese will work, but the smoked Gouda is what I recommend. Not only is it especially tasty, the Gouda retains a sort of creamy texture even at room temperature. This is handy because if you want to serve a variety of appetizers, you can make this first.

---

1 Tablespoon olive oil
2 small zucchini, shredded (about 2 cups)
2 small cloves garlic, minced
1 jalapeno, stemmed and minced (seeded, if desired)
1 teaspoon dried epazote
Salt and freshly milled black pepper, to taste
4 8-inch flour tortillas, preferably whole wheat
1½ cups (about 3 ounces) grated smoked melting cheese such as Gouda, cheddar or mozzarella
Salsa, for serving, if desired
Sour cream, for serving, if desired

Heat the oil in a medium skillet over medium-high heat. Add the zucchini, garlic, jalapeno and epazote. Cook, stirring often, until the zucchini is cooked through and the mixture becomes dry. Season with salt and pepper to taste. NOTE: Do not salt until after cooking or the zucchini will release liquid and become soggy.

Heat a griddle or cast-iron skillet over medium-high heat. Place one tortilla on the griddle. Spread a quarter of the cheese over it followed by half of the cooked zucchini and another quarter of the cheese. Top with another tortilla and press down. Cook the quesadilla on one side until browned and toasty; use a wide spatula to carefully flip it to the other side and brown. Remove from the griddle and repeat the process with the remaining ingredients.

To serve, cut each quesadilla into sixths with a pizza wheel or large knife. Serve right away with salsa and sour cream, if using.

Makes 12 pieces

Nutty Cheese Puffs

Crispy on the outside, soft and pillowy on the inside, this is a combination of some of my favorite things. They are terrific as an appetizer, but also make a lovely light lunch when paired with a simple salad. Plain yogurt, made into a cheese, replaces cream cheese here. It must be started 24 hours before making the puffs, so plan accordingly. These reheat surprisingly well. Just pop them in a 400 degree oven for about 10 minutes.

---

1 cup (8 ounces) plain yogurt
$^1/_3$ cup (2 ounces) crumbled Gorgonzola cheese (avoid using "creamy" style)
$^1/_2$ cup (1 ounce) minced arugula
$^1/_4$ cup finely chopped toasted walnuts or filberts
Salt and freshly milled black pepper, to taste
20 sheets phyllo dough
$^1/_4$ cup olive oil

Drain the yogurt to make a cheese by placing it in a cheesecloth-lined strainer suspended over a bowl to catch the dripping liquid. Cover and place in refrigerator for at least 24 hours. Discard the liquids.

Preheat the oven to 425 degrees.

Combine the yogurt cheese with the Gorgonzola, arugula, nuts, salt and pepper.

To assemble each puff: Brush one sheet of phyllo dough lightly with olive oil. Top with a second sheet of dough; brush again with oil. (As you work, keep the unused phyllo covered with a towel to prevent it from drying out.) Place 1 Tablespoon of the cheese mixture in one corner of the sheets of phyllo. Fold sheets in half, lengthwise to cover the cheese; fold the cheese-covered corner over at an angle to form a triangle. Keep folding, each time at an angle continuing the triangle.

Tuck the extra length of phyllo under and place the puffs with that side down onto an oiled baking sheet and brush tops with more olive oil. (The recipe can be prepared ahead to this point: cover and refrigerate up to 8 hours.) Bake 10 to 12 minutes or until the cheese puffs are golden. Serve warm but not piping hot from the oven.

Makes 10

Herbed Ricotta Spread

Full-fat ricotta gives the best flavor in this dish. If you want to use a low-fat product, strain away the extra water by suspending the ricotta, covered, in a cheesecloth-lined strainer overnight. Consider using any extra spread for a terrific omelet filling.

---

1 container (15 ounces) ricotta cheese
5 teaspoons chopped fresh oregano
5 teaspoons snipped fresh chives
4 teaspoons chopped fresh flat-leaf parsley
1 teaspoon kosher salt
$\frac{1}{8}$ teaspoon coarsely ground black pepper
$\frac{1}{8}$ teaspoon freshly grated nutmeg
Parsley leaves, for garnish, if desired
Crackers, bread or fresh vegetables, for serving

Combine the cheese with the chopped herbs, salt, pepper and nutmeg. Cover and refrigerate for at least an hour.

If desired, form the cheese spread into a mound and decorate with whole leaves of parsley.

Serve with crackers, bread or fresh vegetables.

Makes 2 cups

SAVORY ASIDE

Themed Pots.

No room for a full blown in-the-ground herb garden? Consider planting your favorites in a decorative pot for the patio.

Herbs that are used in your favorite cuisines are a natural for planting together since that's how they grow in nature.

May I offer a few themed combinations? French: tarragon, chervil, parsley, thyme and rosemary; Italian: basil, marjoram, rosemary, oregano and parsley; Mexican: cilantro, chiles and Mexican oregano; Greek: oregano, mint, garlic and dill; or even a salad pot with arugula, garlic, fennel and parsley.

Three Layer Cheese Ball

This recipe makes one large cheese ball that is great for a crowd. If your gathering is smaller, say six or eight people, you might want to cut the recipe in half or make two balls. I like to make three or four of these around the holidays for last minute gifts or entertaining. It's an impressive presentation that is easy to achieve. People always want to know where I bought it.

___

2 cups (16 ounces) cream cheese, softened, divided
1/2 cup (3 ounces) crumbled Gorgonzola cheese
1 cup (4 ounces) finely shredded sharp cheddar cheese
1 teaspoon smoked Spanish paprika
1/2 teaspoon dry mustard
1 teaspoon dried dill weed
1/8 teaspoon cayenne
1 1/2 cups chopped walnuts, toasted

Mix 1/4 cup of the cream cheese with the Gorgonzola; shape into a ball. Place on a waxed paper-lined plate, transfer to the freezer and chill while preparing the next layer.

Combine the cheddar cheese with 3/4 cup of the cream cheese, the paprika and dry mustard. Remove the Gorgonzola ball from the freezer and press the cheddar mixture around it, maintaining the round shape. Return to freezer while preparing the next layer.

Mix the dill weed and cayenne into the remaining cream cheese. Again, work this mixture onto the ball of other cheeses, maintaining the roundness.

Place the toasted walnuts on a sheet of waxed paper. Roll the cheese ball in the nuts to coat well, pressing them gently into the cheese.

Serve right away with crackers or wrap well in plastic and keep in the refrigerator for up to one week. Bring to room temperature before serving.

Makes 1

Toasted Ravioli

This snack you often find on bar menus isn't all that difficult to make at home. Yes, the pasta is fried, but you can get away with less oil than you may think, and you can drain away more of the fat than the fry cook does by transferring the pasta to paper towels before serving. Look for fresh ravioli in the dairy case at the supermarket or check the refrigerated section of the produce department for fancy gourmet varieties. Your favorite ranch-style dressing is another tasty option as a dipping sauce, especially if you choose a veggie-filled ravioli.

---

2 large eggs
2 teaspoons no-salt Italian herb blend
¾ cup fine dry breadcrumbs
One package (approximately 10 ounces) fresh ravioli
About ½ cup peanut oil
Marinara sauce, heated, for dipping

Beat the eggs with the Italian herbs in a wide, shallow bowl. Place the breadcrumbs on a large sheet of waxed paper. To bread the ravioli, dip each one first into the beaten egg; allow excess to drip off then transfer the pasta to the breadcrumbs. Press the crumbs onto the ravioli, shaking lightly to remove the excess. (Using one hand for the egg mixture and the other for the bread-crumbs helps keep your hands neater.) Hold the breaded ravioli on a wire rack until you have finished coating all of them.

Pour enough oil into an 8-inch sauté pan to reach a depth of about ¼-inch; heat over medium high until the surface shimmers but the oil isn't smoking. Test to see if it is ready for frying by dropping in a large breadcrumb; if it sizzles and rises to the surface you are set to go. Fry 3 or 4 of the breaded ravioli at a time, depending on size, by gently nudging them into the oil to avoid splashing. Once browned, after a minute or so, use a slotted spoon to carefully turn them over and brown the other side, another minute to 90 seconds. Transfer to double layers of paper toweling to drain. Continue frying the remaining breaded ravioli. You may need to adjust the temperature of your burner down as the oil continues to heat.

Arrange the fried ravioli on a serving plate with a shallow dish of the warm pasta sauce for dipping.

Serves 2 or 3

Za'atar-Tomato Appetizer

Za'atar is a Middle Eastern spice blend often used in yogurt or to season bread. Here it pairs perfectly with cherry tomatoes, the smaller the better for perching on planks of flatbread. If you have some of the seasoning left over, sock it away in your spice cabinet for sprinkling on boiled eggs, cucumbers or toast later. Look for sumac at Middle Eastern markets or well-stocked spice shops.

---

2 teaspoons white sesame seeds
2 Tablespoons dried thyme
1 Tablespoon sumac
½ teaspoon salt
1 pint (12 ounces) small cherry tomatoes
1 recipe Chickpea Flatbread (page 68) or other fresh flatbread

Toast the sesame seeds by shaking them in a dry skillet over medium-high heat until they are slightly browned and aromatic. Allow to cool on a plate before using.

In a small container with a lid, shake together the toasted sesame seeds, thyme, sumac and salt. This creates a Middle Eastern spice blend called "za'atar."

Cut each of the cherry tomatoes in half placing them into a medium bowl as you go. Sprinkle with one Tablespoon of the za'atar; toss well. Taste and add more of the seasoning, in small increments, until you have what you consider a tasty concoction. Serve right away with the flatbread, allowing diners to pile the tomatoes onto the bread for themselves.

Makes enough for 4 to 6, depending on serving size

Bacon and Thyme Stuffed Tomatoes

Here's the perfect dish for a potluck or the next time it's your turn to bring a treat. The tomatoes look cheery arranged on a plate and the taste is familiar yet unexpected. People are often surprised to discover that thyme is the "secret ingredient." The tomatoes are best when filled within hours before serving.

$1/2$ pound sliced bacon, cut into thin strips
$2/3$ cup finely minced red onion
1 Tablespoon fresh thyme leaves, chopped, plus more for garnish
1 package (8 ounces) cream cheese, at room temperature
$1/4$ teaspoon salt
$1/8$ teaspoon freshly milled black pepper
1 pint (12 ounces) cherry tomatoes

Cook the bacon over medium heat until crisp. Use a slotted spoon to transfer the cooked bacon onto paper toweling to drain; discard all but 2 teaspoons of the bacon fat. Wipe down the outside edges of the pan to prevent smoking and return the pan to the heat; add the red onion. Cook, stirring often, until the onion is softened but not browned. Mix in the thyme, cook another minute and remove from heat. Allow to cool before proceeding.

Chop the cooked bacon even finer and place in a medium bowl with the cream cheese, cooled seasoned onions, salt and pepper. Use a wooden spoon to mix the ingredients thoroughly. Taste; adjust seasonings, if necessary. (This mixture can be made a day or two ahead of time. Wrap well in plastic and store in the refrigerator; bring to room temperature before filling the tomatoes.)

To prepare the tomatoes, slice through each one across the center (as opposed to slicing from stem end to blossom end). Use the small end of a melon baller to remove the seeds. Place, cut sides down, on layers of paper towels to dry slightly.

Fill a standard pastry bag without a tip (or use a sturdy plastic bag and snip off a corner) with the flavored cream cheese. Squeeze a mound, about 2 teaspoons, into each hollowed out tomato shell. Arrange the tomatoes on a serving plate as you go. Sprinkle with the minced thyme and serve right away.

Makes about 50

Corn Cakes with two toppings

My lifelong quest for the perfect corn cake is finally over. That may sound odd, but for years I have tried to come up with one that is tender, not gritty or pasty, and has good flavor. This recipe is based on Mark Bittman's *New York Times* recipe for Arepas with Cheese and Corn. It also incorporates some of the tips I learned watching an arepas Throwdown with Bobby Flay. That's where the corn flour came from and I think it makes a huge difference. I found mine in the natural food section of my supermarket. Corn flour is not cornstarch and it's not cornmeal. A non-stick pan is key here. I started out using a regular pan with lots of oil and the corn cakes still stuck and fell apart. With non-stick cookware, we are able to eliminate the added fat while still achieving a crisp, brown exterior.

1½ cups milk
3 Tablespoons unsalted butter
1½ cups corn flour
¾ teaspoon salt
½ cup (1½ ounces) finely grated cheddar/jack mixed cheese
¾ cup fresh corn kernels (1 large ear) or thawed frozen corn
3 Tablespoons snipped chives
1 small jalapeno, seeded and minced

Heat the milk with the butter over medium heat until the butter is melted and the milk is steaming.

Meanwhile, toss the corn flour with the salt and cheese in a medium mixing bowl. Pour in the hot milk and stir well. Mix in the corn, chives and jalapeno. Set aside to rest for about 15 minutes. Stir again, the batter will be thick.

Heat a non-stick griddle or other large pan over medium-high heat. Working in batches, drop the batter by ¼-cup increments, pressing down with the back of a spoon to make patties, onto the hot griddle and cook until golden brown, 3 or 4 minutes; carefully turn over and brown the other side. Continue until all the batter is cooked.

To serve two ways, see the next two recipes for topping options. You can keep the toppings light enough that the cakes can be picked up in hand or treat them like a tostada and load on the toppings. Another way to serve them is to set out all the different toppings and let people come up with their own combinations.

Makes about 12

Poblano-Avocado Topping

This is a super-creamy, super-quick guacamole that works well when combined with a variety of other foods.

1½ avocados, pitted and peeled (use the remaining half as a topping with the black beans, if desired)
1 large poblano chile, roasted then peeled and seeded
¼ teaspoon salt
Corn Cakes (page 18)
4 strips bacon, cooked and crumbled
2 cups shredded romaine lettuce

Puree the avocados with the poblano and the salt in a small food processor. Taste for salt.

Just before serving, spread the corn cakes with a thick layer of the avocado puree, sprinkle with bacon and top with shredded lettuce.

Black Bean and Tomato Topping

This is almost better when made a day before serving. If you do, wait to salt it until just before using so that the tomatoes don't release too much liquid. Adding a bit of cilantro if desired would not be out of place here. Look for the feta-like cotija cheese, sometimes called queso fresco, in the dairy case at supermarkets.

---

1 can (15 ounces) black beans, drained and rinsed
1 ripe tomato, cored and diced
1 teaspoon ground cumin
Splash of olive oil and sherry vinegar
Salt and freshly milled black pepper, to taste
Corn Cakes (page 18)
½ cup sour cream
½ cup crumbled cotija cheese

Toss the black beans with the tomato and cumin. Season with the oil, vinegar, salt and pepper.

Just before serving, spread the corn cakes with a layer of sour cream, a spoonful of the black beans and a sprinkle of the cotija.

.

Onion Tarts

Inspired by an onion tart and glass of wine I enjoyed at a little cafe on my first trip to New York City, this savory snack lets me relive the romantic memory. Think of them for a plated first course or with a salad for a light, elegant lunch.

For the shells:
¾ cup whole wheat pastry flour
½ cup all-purpose flour
½ teaspoon salt
½ cup (1 stick) cold unsalted butter, diced
3-4 Tablespoons ice water

For the filling:
1 Tablespoon unsalted butter
1 Tablespoon olive oil
5 cups (about 1½ lb.) yellow onions, halved and sliced 1/8" thick
¾ teaspoon kosher salt
1 Tablespoon dried thyme leaves
2 Tablespoons dry white wine (or white vermouth)
Freshly milled black pepper

To finish:
1 cup (4 ounces) grated Gruyere cheese
½ cup crème fraiche

To make the shells: In a food processor fitted with the steel blade, pulse the flours and salt to combine. Add the diced butter; pulse 10 to 12 times or until the mixture resembles crumbs. With the machine running, add 3 Tablespoons of the ice water. If the mixture is too dry, add the remaining Tablespoon of water. The dough is ready if it holds together when pinched between your fingers—it may seem a bit dry but try this test before adding more water. Gather the dough, knead briefly to bring together and form into a flattened rectangle about 2-inches thick. Wrap in plastic and allow to rest in the refrigerator at least 30 minutes.

On a lightly floured surface, roll the chilled dough into a 10x16-inch rectangle. Use a pizza wheel to straighten the edges and then cut the dough into 8 squares. Transfer to a parchment-paper lined baking sheet. Return to refrigerator until ready to use.

To make the filling: Melt the butter with the olive oil in a large sauté pan over medium-high heat. Pile in half the onions, sprinkle with half the salt; add the remaining onions and sprinkle with remaining salt. Use a wide spatula to move the onions around to coat them with the salt and melted butter mixture. This is awkward at first but the onions will soon shrink to become more manageable. The onions will also begin to release moisture; once this liquid has evaporated, about 10 minutes, add the thyme and reduce the heat to medium. Continue to cook the onions, stirring frequently, for about 15 minutes more, or until they are very soft and deeply browned. Increase the heat back to medium-high, add the wine; stir the onions and scrape the bottom of the pan to deglaze until the wine evaporates. Remove from heat. Season with black pepper and taste to see if more salt is needed. Cool slightly.

To finish and serve: Preheat the oven to 425 degrees.

Divide the onion filling evenly between the 8 dough squares, arranging in a diagonal strip down the centers from two corners. Top each with a layer of 2 Tablespoons of the grated cheese. Fold the unfilled corners in over the filling so the points are side by side (the dough should not overlap). Bake for 15 to 20 minutes, or until the cheese is bubbly and the crust is nicely browned.

Serve the tarts warm with about 1 Tablespoon of the crème fraiche drizzled over the top.

Makes 8 servings

Individual Eggplant Parmesans

One of my favorite dinner party menus begins with these delicious stacks. Follow them with a second course of pasta tossed with pesto and, for a main dish, serve Renaissance Pork (page 104) with a simple bowl of the freshest lettuce you can find, dressed lightly with olive oil and balsamic vinegar. The star of the show should be the pork but most people will remember the eggplant.

---

6 slices (about ¾-inch thick) from a medium eggplant
¼ cup olive oil
⅓ cup marinara sauce
1 teaspoon dried oregano
6 thick slices (about 6 ounces) of fresh mozzarella
2 Tablespoons freshly grated Parmesan cheese
1 Tablespoon minced fresh flat-leaf parsley, for garnish

Preheat the oven to 450 degrees.

Pour the oil into a pan big enough to hold the eggplant slices in a single layer. Run both sides of the eggplant slices through the oil as you add them to the pan. Roast for 10 minutes, turn each slice over and roast for 10 minutes more. Remove the pan from the oven.

Reset the oven to broil.

Transfer the eggplant slices to a broiler pan. Top each slice with about a Tablespoon of the marinara sauce and a sprinkling of the oregano. Top each with a slice of mozzarella and a sprinkling of the Parmesan.

Place the pan under the broiler. Allow the cheese to melt and become a light toasty brown. Sprinkle with the parsley and serve right away.

Makes 6 servings

Pasta with Spinach Pesto

Rather like a pasta salad, this pretty dish serves well as an appetizer. I like to pack it up for a picnic side dish sometimes. No one would mind if you doubled or tripled the recipe to take along to your next potluck dinner, either.

---

1 cup (4 ounces) small shaped pasta, uncooked
2 Tablespoons Spinach Pesto (page 213)
1 large ripe tomato, cored and diced
1½ cups (½ pound) finely chopped steamed broccoli crowns
¼ teaspoon salt
⅛ teaspoon freshly milled black pepper
¼ cup chopped toasted walnuts, for garnish

Cook the pasta according to package directions but see the next step before draining.

Place the spinach pesto into a deep serving bowl. Just before draining the pasta, dilute the pesto with 2 Tablespoons of the cooking water; stir together. Drain the pasta and add to the bowl with the pesto, tossing lightly to coat. Gently stir in the tomato, broccoli, salt and the pepper. Taste and adjust seasonings, as necessary. Sprinkle with the walnuts. Serve warm or at room temperature.

Makes 2 ample servings

Festive Fruit Platter with Poppy Seed Dip

This recipe dates back to my days of cooking at a fraternity house. It was the perfect appetizer or brunch addition when the guys had ladies in for special events.

---

2 cups vanilla yogurt
2 Tablespoons frozen orange juice concentrate, thawed
2 Tablespoons poppy seeds
1 cantaloupe
1 bunch seedless green grapes
1 bunch seedless red grapes
Juice of 1 lemon
1 red apple
1 yellow apple
2 oranges
3 kiwi fruits
18 strawberries

Combine the yogurt, orange juice concentrate and poppy seeds in a bowl. Set aside.

Cut the stem end from each side of the cantaloupe to make flat surfaces. Use a pencil to draw a zig-zag line around the center of the melon, horizontal to the cut ends, and use this line as a guide to cut a decorative edge in the melon halves. Scoop out the seeds and most of the flesh to make a serving bowl for the yogurt. Discard the seeds and save the flesh for another use. Fill each cantaloupe half with the yogurt dip. Cover one with plastic wrap and store in refrigerator to use as needed later. Place the other yogurt-filled half in the center of a large serving platter.

Cut the grapes into small bunches with a sharp pair of scissors. Arrange half of the grape bunches decoratively around the base of the cantaloupe on the serving platter. Set aside the remaining grapes for later use.

Combine the lemon juice with 2 cups of cold water in a large bowl. Core and seed the apples and slice them into ½-inch wedges. Place apple wedges into the lemon water for a minute or two and then drain—this will keep them from discoloring. Arrange them in alternating colors, rows radiating out from the cantaloupe and grapes on both sides.

Peel the oranges and remove as much of the white membrane as possible. Divide into sections and arrange next to the apples on each side, again radiating out from the center.

Peel and slice the kiwi into wedges and arrange on the platter in the same fashion.

Wash the strawberries, leaving the stems on. Place berries around the edges of the kiwi. Use the remaining grapes to fill any gaps on the platter.

Serve immediately or cover with plastic wrap and hold in the refrigerator for no longer than 2 hours. Chill any fruit that did not fit on the platter. Use extra fruit, as well as the other yogurt filled cantaloupe, to replenish the platter as necessary.

Makes 2 cups dip and a party tray for 6 to 8

All-American Five Onion Soup, page 38

Soups and Stews: Enticing concoctions from around the world

Soups and stews could be considered the perfect meal. A healthy mixture all in one pot and ready when needed, soup is an important element of any cooks' repertoire. The fact that there are usually leftovers only adds to the attraction.

Whenever I am expecting company from out of town, I like to greet them with a simmering pot of veggies and beans or a savory stew of meat and potatoes. Add a basket of bread and a simple dessert for a no-fuss meal that gets you out of the kitchen fast, giving you time to visit.

The recipes in this chapter are hearty and highly spiced. It is important to taste as you go, adjusting the seasonings to achieve a proper balance with the other ingredients you are using. With a few exceptions, perhaps the most fundamental component of a soup is a good stock.

In a perfect world you would make that stock from scratch every time. Simmering roasted beef or chicken bones with just the right amount of water, vegetables and seasonings is certainly a worthwhile weekend project. But, there are times when we are rushed and need to reach for something quick. Cans of broth and cubes of bouillon are perfectly acceptable—as long as you keep high-quality products on hand. Take the time to consider which ones you like the best.

It is a good idea to look for those with a low-sodium content as they will reduce a bit, increasing in saltiness, while cooking. I find the broth pastes available in jars are a handy item to have around. As a general rule, however, I keep Swanson's chicken stock on hand.

Soups and stews are highly amenable to fresh or dried herbs. While many of these recipes call for dried herbs, by all means use fresh if they are available, just add them closer to the end of the cooking time. A combination of fresh and dried herbs adds an interesting dimension to soups. The Meatball Minestrone is an excellent example of this. Dried herbs are simmered along with the vegetables and beans giving a hearty undertone to the soup. A good handful of fresh herbs tossed in just before serving adds brightness.

SAVORY ASIDE

Watch for MSG.

Monosodium glutamate, MSG, is a flavor enhancer to which some people are sensitive. A complicated chemical compound, it is best described as a substance that makes your tastebuds stand up so that they are more receptive to flavors. Although the U.S Food and Drug Administration recognizes it as safe, I avoid it on the basis that it is just another additive I don't really need to ingest. Besides, my food tastes good without it! The FDA does demand that it be identified on labels. This has led to MSG listed in the disguise of yeast extract or whey protein, or even just "natural flavor" on the ingredient lists of food products and some herb and spice blends. It is worth investigating further if you wish to avoid MSG.

One handy trick for enhancing dried seasonings is to chop them along with a bit of fresh parsley. If fresh cilantro isn't available, for instance, sprinkle dried coriander over fresh parsley before mincing it. I do it this way all the time because I don't like cilantro.

Perhaps you are already aware that coriander is the seed of the cilantro plant. Many people, including me, have a serious aversion to cilantro, saying it tastes of soap. I find the somewhat earthy, lemony taste of coriander much more palatable. Cilantro as a dried herb is a poor alternative to the fresh leaves because it retains very little of the essential oils that give herbs their zing.

Depth of flavor also comes from adding the same seasonings at different times during the cooking process, as in the Yankee Cajun Gumbo. The Cajun spice blend is sprinkled over the aromatics in the initial sauté, added with the stock next, and then seasoned to perfection just before serving time.

Cajun seasoning blends are complex combinations of peppers, paprika and other spices that vary by manufacturer. Look for the ones that don't contain salt. Cajun blends are often too salty and, since salt weighs more than the other ingredients, not particularly economical for you.

Commercial chili powder makes one of two appearances in this chapter in the Award Winning Green Chili recipe. With so many peppers, chiles and flavors in this recipe, everyday chili powder makes sense. No spice cabinet would be complete without some sort of chili powder just because it's such a handy way to add flavor in a flash. As always, look for the best quality blend you can find and make sure it is one without salt or MSG. A typical blend will contain ground chiles, of course, along with cumin, oregano and other "secret" ingredients.

The noble bay leaf is common to long-simmering stews. A single dried leaf gives a subtle scent and an ever so slight bitterness that enhances the other ingredients in the pot. They are unpleasant to bite into, however, and have been proven a choking hazard, so remove bay leaves before serving.

If your climate permits, try growing a *Laurus nobilis*, or bay tree. They can take the cold to about 20 degrees (F). If your temperatures drop below this, consider planting one in a pot that you can easily move around to provide necessary protection. Fresh bay leaves are a bit more intense in flavor than dried.

As wonderful as soup is for a main dish, consider serving just a cup of it as an appetizer. This is the traditional way to serve goulash in Hungary. The All-American Five Onion Soup, flavorful but not heavy, is just right as a starter. The more hearty Soup of Pasta and Garbanzos would segue well into a main dish salad.

I've never been a big fan of cold soups, but the Fruit Gazpacho is my exception. I love the elegance of it and the surprise it becomes when presented as a dessert. The simple grating of nutmeg over each serving is the only enhancement this combination of fresh fruits needs.

Soups and stews offer the creative cook a nearly blank canvas. Endless variations can be derived from the recipes in this chapter. Beans are interchangeable, different varieties of chiles become available at different times; the herbs you have on hand will most likely be just the seasoning you want. When you cook with what is fresh, you can't go wrong.

Fruit Gazpacho

Fruit salad gets a makeover. More elegant than mixed fruit, this chilled soup serves as a light dessert or an unusual addition to brunch. The silky base, a puree of cantaloupe, banana and orange juice, is amenable to any combination of fresh fruits, regardless of the season. For an attractive presentation, choose a wide variety of colors in the mixed fruit and cut them all roughly the same size. This should be prepared no more than one day in advance.

---

1 large, ripe cantaloupe
1 large, ripe banana, peeled
½ cup orange juice
3 cups mixed fresh fruit chunks, such as apples or pears, cored and chopped; plums, peaches or nectarines, pitted and chopped; oranges, peeled, sectioned, seeded and halved; blueberries or grapes; kiwi fruit, peeled and chopped; or anything that is fresh
½ cup plain or vanilla yogurt, for garnish
4 slices starfruit, for garnish
Freshly grated nutmeg, for garnish

Cut the cantaloupe in half; remove seeds. Place cut sides down on a cutting board and carefully trim off the rind with a sharp knife. Cut the peeled cantaloupe halves into large chunks.

Place the peeled cantaloupe chunks, banana and orange juice into the bowl of a food processor fitted with steel blade. Process on low speed until smooth, about 2 minutes. Place a fine mesh sieve over a 4-cup measure and strain the puree through the sieve. Use a wooden spoon to push the liquids into the measuring cup. Continue until you have about 2½ cups of liquid. (You will be left with a pulp that is the consistency of applesauce. Set this aside or it eat right away, it is delicious.)

Add the 3 cups of mixed fruit to the cantaloupe/banana mixture; stir gently. Cover and chill for at least 30 minutes.

Divide the fruit gazpacho between four chilled bowls, allowing about 1 cup per serving. Top each with a dollop of 2 Tablespoons of yogurt and a starfruit slice. Sprinkle with nutmeg. Serve immediately.

Makes 4 servings

Julia's Leek and Potato Soup

After I read *The United States of Arugula,* by David Kamp, I felt compelled to dive into my *From Julia Child's Kitchen* cookbook. The first recipe in the book is for a potato and leek soup. She offers so many variations and possible additions that I've condensed what has evolved as my favorite into the recipe below. Grating the potatoes instead of cubing them is my own idea. I adore the resulting texture. To avoid having them turn brown, grate them while the leeks are sautéing in the butter. And, please note the two separate additions of the two different parts of the leeks. Serve this as is on the first day and then add bits of leftover vegetables, ham or anything else that strikes your fancy the next day.

---

3 Tablespoons unsalted butter
3 cups sliced leeks, white part only
3 Tablespoons all-purpose flour
6 cups hot water
3½ cups (about 4 medium or 1½ pounds) peeled and shredded baking potatoes
1 cup of the tender green parts of the leeks, minced
1 Tablespoon salt
Freshly milled black pepper, to taste
2 cups milk
½ cup half-and-half
Snipped chives for garnish

Melt the butter over medium heat in a soup kettle. Stir in the 3 cups leeks, cover the pan and cook slowly for 5 minutes without browning. Blend in the flour; cook and stir over medium heat for 2 minutes to cook the flour without browning it. Remove from heat, let cool for a moment and gradually beat in a cup of the hot water. Blend thoroughly with the flour and leeks then stir in the remaining water. Stir in the salt and pepper, green parts of the leeks and

SAVORY ASIDE

Banish the gritty leek.

When cooking with leeks take care to wash them well since sand has a tendency to get bound up within the many layers of the vegetable. Start by trimming off the root end and the tough green leaves, usually three or four inches from the white. Now cut the leek in half lengthwise and examine it for dirt. Sometimes you can simply hold the halves under running water and fan the layers to wash away the grit. Especially dirty leeks may require that you cut them as needed for the recipe and then give them a good soak in a bowl of cold water. Swish them around a bit, then lift the leeks from the water. The sand will settle to the bottom of the bowl. Do this more than once if you still see, or feel, grit on the leeks.

the potatoes. Bring to a boil, reduce heat to a simmer and cook, partially covered for about 40 minutes, or until the vegetables are thoroughly tender. *(Soup may be made ahead to this point. Allow to cool, cover and refrigerate. Bring it to a simmer before adding the milk.)*

Just before serving, blend in the milk and half-and-half. Taste carefully for salt and pepper, adding more if needed. Ladle into bowls, garnish with the chives and serve piping hot.

Makes 8 cups

Tomato-Tortellini Soup

In the time it takes to open a can of soup, you can whip up something far more palatable. This fast and simple soup works with any type of tortellini, meat or cheese, fresh or frozen, but I have enjoyed it the most using fresh pasta that I find in the supermarket dairy case. Freshly-snipped herbs like basil, oregano, rosemary and/or thyme from the garden could certainly replace the commercial Italian blend. If you have this option, use about 3 Tablespoons fresh herbs and add them halfway through the cooking of the tortellini. My Italian herbs include red pepper flakes so if I'm using fresh herbs I still like to add a sprinkling of those, too. If you are planning to prepare this recipe for just yourself with the idea of leftovers for tomorrow, you might want to cook only half the tortellini in the broth each time. This will prevent the pasta from getting soggy as it sits overnight.

---

1 can (15 ounces) diced tomatoes in juice
1 can (15 ounces) chicken stock (or 2 cups homemade broth)
1 Tablespoon Italian herbs blend
1½ to 2 cups (12 ounces) fresh or frozen tortellini
2 Tablespoons freshly shredded Parmesan cheese, for garnish, if desired

Combine the tomatoes, stock, ½ cup water and the herbs in a 3-quart saucepan over medium-high heat; bring to a boil. Add the tortellini and adjust the heat to maintain a strong simmer. Cook as directed on the pasta package.

Ladle into warmed bowls, sprinkle with a bit of the cheese and serve immediately.

Serves 4 as a first course or 2 as a main dish

SAVORY ASIDE

Fresh ginger on demand.

"Hands" of ginger are available year around at most supermarkets. You need only break off the amount you wish to buy. It's best stored unwrapped in the vegetable bin of your refrigerator if you use it frequently. If you want to store it longer than a week or so, cut it into 1-inch lengths (unpeeled), wrap them individually, put them into a freezer bag and freeze them. Ginger defrosts quickly, so you'll have it when you need it.

Sesame Noodle Soup

This satisfying take on chicken noodle soup is a cinch to prepare despite the long list of ingredients. Tamari is a lower sodium version of soy sauce. Look for edamame, aka fresh soy beans, in the frozen food aisle. You can buy them in the pod, which are fun to eat as a snack, or already shelled and recipe-ready. A bit of cooked chicken or cubes of tofu wouldn't be out of place here, if you're looking for additional protein.

---

5 green onions, see instructions for preparation
1 Tablespoon unsalted butter
1 large carrot, minced (about ½ cup)
1 rib celery, minced (about ¼ cup)
1-inch length fresh ginger root, peeled and minced (3 teaspoons)
1 fat garlic clove, minced (scant Tablespoon)
1 Tablespoon tamari, plus more for passing at table
3½ cups chicken stock
$1/_3$ cup vermicelli noodles or tiny pasta shapes
½ cup shelled edamame
Freshly milled black pepper, to taste
2-4 teaspoons toasted sesame oil, plus more for passing at table

Mince the white part and about 2 inches of the green tops of the onions. You should have about $1/_3$ cup. Slice remaining green tops for garnish.

Melt the butter in a 3-quart saucepan over medium heat. Add the minced green onions, carrot, celery, ginger and garlic. Cook, stirring almost constantly to avoid burning the garlic and ginger, for about 5 minutes. Stir the tamari into the chicken stock and pour over the vegetables in the pan; bring the soup to a boil. Add the noodles and edamame, return to a boil and then reduce heat to maintain a strong simmer, for about 6 minutes or as long as the noodle package directs. Season with the black pepper.

To serve, ladle the soup into warmed bowls, drizzle each with 1 teaspoon of the sesame oil and a good pinch of the sliced green onion tops. Serve immediately, passing additional tamari and sesame oil at the table.

Makes 2 to 4 servings

Soup of Pasta and Garbanzos

Plenty of pasta and bean soup recipes exist, but I love the simple yet delicious taste of this combination. Just the aroma of the onion, garlic and oregano sautéing sets my mouth to watering in anticipation. Fresh oregano gives the soup a bitterness, I definitely prefer dried for this application. The recipe is written to serve four as an appetizer or accompaniment to a main dish. If you want to serve it as a main dish, just divide this between two bowls rather than four or double the recipe.

---

1 can (15 ounces) garbanzo beans, rinsed, drained and divided
1 Tablespoon olive oil
¾ cup finely chopped onion
1 clove garlic, minced
1 teaspoon dried oregano
1 cup canned chopped tomatoes, with juice
2 cups beef stock
¾ cup (about 2 ounces) small-shaped pasta (like sea shells)
¼ teaspoon crushed red pepper, if desired
Salt and freshly milled black pepper, to taste
¼ cup extra-virgin olive oil, for serving
¼ cup freshly grated Parmesan cheese, for serving

As you begin the soup, bring a large pot of salted water to a boil for cooking the pasta. Place half the can of garbanzo beans into a small bowl and mash them with a fork.

Heat the olive oil over medium-high heat in a 2-quart saucepan. Add the onion; cook and stir for 2 minutes. Stir in the garlic and oregano, cook and stir 1 minute more. Add the tomatoes; reduce heat to medium and cook 3 to 5 minutes or until most of the liquid has evaporated. Stir in the beef broth and the mashed garbanzo beans. Maintain the soup at a simmer until the pasta is finished cooking.

After the pasta water has come to a boil, add the pasta and cook according to package directions.

Just before draining the pasta, stir the remaining whole garbanzo beans into the soup along with the crushed red pepper, if using. Taste; season with salt and pepper, as needed. Stir in the drained, cooked pasta.

Divide the soup between four shallow bowls. Drizzle each with 1 Tablespoon extra-virgin olive oil and sprinkle each serving with 1 Tablespoon of the cheese and serve immediately.

Makes 4 servings

All-American Five Onion Soup

Sour cream makes an attractive garnish to this hearty yet still light soup. If desired, top each serving with a small dollop of sour cream and then sprinkle with the chives. Sausage and Sage Corn Muffins (page 56) are terrific alongside steaming bowls of this soup.

---

1 Tablespoon unsalted butter
1 Tablespoon olive oil
1 yellow onion, peeled, halved and sliced thin (2 cups)
1 red onion, peeled, halved and sliced thin (2 cups)
2 shallots, minced (1 cup)
1 leek, washed, sliced including 2 inches of the green part (2 cups)
6 green onions, sliced, including but keeping separate the green parts (2 Tablespoons white portion, 3 Tablespoons green)
2 Tablespoons minced fresh thyme, or 2 teaspoons dried
¼ cup dry red wine
1¼ cups beef stock
1¼ cups chicken stock
½ teaspoon salt
¼ teaspoon freshly milled black pepper
2 Tablespoons snipped chives, for garnish

In a 3-quart saucepan over medium-high heat, melt the butter with the olive oil. Add the yellow and red onions; stir well. Cook for 5 minutes, stirring often. Add the shallots and leek. Cook and stir for another 5 minutes and then add the white parts of the green onions and thyme. Reduce the heat to medium and cook, stirring frequently, until the onions are well browned, about 15 minutes. Raise the heat and deglaze the pan by pouring in the wine, stirring and scraping the bottom of the pot until the liquid has evaporated. Add the beef and chicken stocks, salt and pepper. Bring to a boil, reduce heat and simmer another 10 minutes. Stir in the sliced green parts of the green onions.

Just before serving, ladle the soup into four heated serving bowls and sprinkle with the snipped chives. Serve piping hot.

Makes 4 servings

Curried Squash Soup

This is one of those recipes that happen when you transform leftovers into something so tasty that it must be duplicated. If you roast the squash ahead of time, the hearty soup can be prepared in just minutes. Add a bit more stock and/or milk if you prefer a somewhat thinner soup. The walnut oil and pumpkin seeds may seem like a garnish, but they actually complement the other flavors well. Both are available at most supermarkets.

---

1 acorn squash
1 teaspoon olive oil
Kosher salt and freshly milled black pepper
1 Tablespoon unsalted butter
1 shallot, minced (about ¼ cup)
2 teaspoons curry powder
1 cup chicken stock
¼ cup milk
½ teaspoon salt
1 teaspoon walnut oil
2 Tablespoons roasted pepitas (pumpkin seeds)

Preheat the oven to 450 degrees. Carefully cut the squash in half lengthwise and scrape out the seeds. Brush the flesh with the olive oil; season with salt and pepper. Place the squash halves, cut side up, into a baking dish that will just hold them. Roast in the oven for 45 minutes or until deeply browned and quite tender. Remove from the oven and set aside to cool. When the squash has cooled enough to handle, use a wooden spoon to scrape the flesh from the shell. Puree the roasted flesh in a food processor until smooth.

Melt the butter in a 2-quart saucepan over medium-high heat. Add the shallot; sauté for 2-3 minutes, until tender. Sprinkle with the curry powder and cook, stirring constantly, for another minute. Add the roasted squash puree and chicken stock. Reduce the heat; stir in the milk and salt and simmer for a few minutes to heat through. Taste for salt and pepper, adjusting as you like.

Divide the soup between two bowls. Drizzle the tops with ½ teaspoon each of the walnut oil and sprinkle each with a Tablespoon of the pepitas.

Makes 2 servings

Vaquero Stew

This thick and satisfying soup can be spiced up with hot Italian sausage and Pepper-Jack cheese if you are looking for some extra heat. Hominy is a "puffed-up" corn product that adds a toothsome quality to the stew. Seek it out if you have never used it but, if it's unavailable, try using both yellow and white corn instead.

½ pound Italian sausage, casings removed (if necessary)
3 Tablespoons unsalted butter
1 medium yellow onion, chopped
3 Tablespoons all-purpose flour
2 cups chicken stock
2 cups fresh or frozen corn kernels, thawed
1 can (15 ounces) hominy, rinsed and drained
1 can (4 ounces) diced green chiles
2 teaspoons ground cumin
¼ teaspoon salt
$\frac{1}{8}$ teaspoon freshly milled black pepper
4 drops hot pepper sauce, or to taste
1 cup (4 ounces) shredded Monterrey Jack cheese, plus 1 Tablespoon for garnish
1 small ripe tomato, cored and diced, for garnish

Cook the sausage in a 3-quart saucepan over medium-high heat, stirring frequently, until it begins to brown, about 5 minutes. (Don't worry if it sticks a little to the pan, we'll deal with that later.) Transfer to a paper-towel lined plate to drain; set aside. Pour off any grease that has accumulated in the pan.

Return the pan to the heat and add the butter. After the butter has melted, add the onion and cook, stirring frequently, until translucent, about 5 minutes. Stir in the flour one Tablespoon at a time. Cook and stir 2-3 minutes or until the mixture takes on a caramel color. Slowly stir in the chicken stock, scraping the bottom of the pan to loosen any sticky bits that will add flavor. Bring to a boil; cook, stirring constantly, until mixture begins to thicken. Add the cooked sausage, corn, hominy, green chiles, cumin, salt, pepper and hot sauce. Stir well. Return to a boil; reduce heat to low. Simmer for 10 minutes, stirring occasionally. Remove from heat; stir in the one cup cheese until melted.

To serve, ladle about 1¼ cups of the stew into each of four bowls. Garnish each bowl with a quarter of the diced tomato and a sprinkling of the remaining cheese. Serve immediately.

Makes 4 servings

Award Winning Green Chili

This recipe won first prize at a chili cook-off in the "vegetarian" category. It's good as a spicy stew, but I like to use it as a sauce for other tasty Mexican dishes like seafood enchiladas or huevos rancheros. Another option is to add a bit of cooked pork and some hominy for a spicy posole. By the way, if you want to try the winner of the main event "bowl of red" category, check out My Best Chili (page 43).

---

2 Tablespoons olive oil
1 large yellow onion, chopped
1 green bell pepper, cored, seeded and chopped
2 cloves garlic, minced
2 teaspoons chili powder
1 teaspoon dried Mexican oregano
1 can (15 ounces) diced tomatoes in juice
2 cans (4 ounces each) diced green chiles
¼ cup sliced pickled jalapenos, chopped, plus 1 Tablespoon of the juice
¼ cup diced roasted red peppers
½ teaspoon salt
½ cup water
$1/8$ to ¼ teaspoon crushed red pepper, optional for really hot stuff

Heat the oil in a 3-quart saucepan over medium-high heat. Add the onion and bell pepper. Stir well and cook, stirring regularly, for about 5 minutes or until softened and browned a bit. Add the garlic, chile powder and oregano; cook and stir for a minute. Stir in the tomatoes, green chiles, jalapenos with their juice, roasted red peppers, salt and water. Bring to a boil then reduce the heat to medium-low. Cover and simmer for at least 15 minutes. If time allows, simmer for about an hour. Stir in the crushed red pepper, if using, or pass it at the table.

Makes 4 cups

SAVORY ASIDE

Mexican oregano.

Greek oregano is as essential to pizza as Mexican oregano is to chili powder. You may use the two types interchangeably, but using a specific one increases the authenticity of certain dishes. Mexican oregano has a more rustic flavor with less hint of mint in the aroma. Use it for your Mexican cooking. Set the two varieties side by side and you will quickly see the difference. Mexican oregano has an abundance of what appear to be tiny flower buds and leaves while Greek oregano has a more cut-leaf appearance.

My Best Chili

Coriander symbolizes hidden worth. That's why I look at it as the secret ingredient in my chili that everyone seems to love. For extra flavor, use two different types of ground chile. For many years I used canned tomato sauce in this recipe. Once, when I was out of sauce, I used diced tomatoes in juice and I've never gone back. It's easy to puree the tomatoes with a handheld blender. Mom's Cornbread (page 225) is almost mandatory with this chili. An added bonus, it freezes really well.

1½ pounds ground beef
1 large yellow onion, chopped
1 medium green bell pepper, cored, seeded and chopped
1 Tablespoon ground New Mexican chile, divided
1 Tablespoon ground cumin, divided
2 teaspoons Mexican oregano, divided
1½ teaspoons salt, divided
1 teaspoon ground coriander, divided
¼ teaspoon freshly milled black pepper, divided
2 bay leaves, divided
2 cans (15 ounces) chili beans in sauce
1 can (28 ounces) diced tomato in juice, pureed smooth
Dash cayenne
3 Tablespoons dried parsley

Brown the ground beef in a soup kettle over medium-high heat; drain off fat. Add the onion and bell pepper, 2 teaspoons of the chile, 2 teaspoons of the cumin, 1 teaspoon of the oregano, ½ teaspoon of the coriander, ½ teaspoon of the salt, $\frac{1}{8}$ of a teaspoon of the black pepper and 1 of the bay leaves. Mix well and cook, stirring regularly to prevent the spices from burning, for about 5 minutes, or until the vegetables are softened.

Add the chili beans and tomatoes. Rinse each of the cans with ¼ cup of water and pour into chili. Stir in the remaining 1 teaspoon each of the chile and cumin, the 1 teaspoon of oregano, ½ teaspoon of coriander, 1 teaspoon of salt, the $\frac{1}{8}$ teaspoon of black pepper and the other bay leaf as well as the dash of cayenne and the parsley. Bring to a boil; reduce heat. Simmer at least 15 minutes, the longer the better. Remove the bay leaves before serving.

Makes 6 to 8 servings

Split Pea Stew with Savory, Bacon and Onion

Savory, the bean herb, is one of our most underused seasonings. You'll find it dried alongside other herbs and spices at the supermarket, but I encourage you to grow a plant for a steady supply. Two varieties exist—summer and winter. When using it fresh follow this rule: Summer savory is snipped and chopped, while the leaves of winter savory should be stripped from the stems like rosemary. Cooking times for dried beans vary with the age of the product. You may need to cook your split peas a little less or a little more than the times listed here.

---

1 cup (8 ounces) dried split peas
4 cups water
1 medium yellow onion, minced, divided
1 bay leaf
1 large carrot, chopped
1 teaspoon salt
2 Tablespoons minced fresh savory, or 2 teaspoons dried, divided
$1/8$ teaspoon freshly milled black pepper, or to taste
½ pound sliced bacon, cut into thin strips

In a 3-quart saucepan combine the split peas, water, half of the minced onion and the bay leaf. Bring to a boil over high heat. Reduce the heat to medium, or just enough to maintain a strong simmer, and cook for 30 minutes. Stir in the chopped carrot, salt and 1 Tablespoon of the savory. Simmer 15 minutes more. Stir in the black pepper; then continue cooking until the carrots are tender. (*Can be made ahead to this point. The stew will thicken up as it cools, add a bit more water when reheating.*)

While the peas are simmering, cook the bacon until nearly crisp. Drain off all but 1 Tablespoon of the fat. Add the other half of the onion and the remaining 1 Tablespoon savory. Cook and stir frequently until the bacon is crisp and the onion is a deep golden brown, watching carefully toward the end of cooking as it can burn quickly. Drain off the fat and set aside until the stew is ready.

To serve, reserve ¼ cup of the cooked bacon and onion mixture and stir the rest into the stew; taste and adjust seasonings. Remove the bay leaves. Ladle into bowls. Garnish with 1 Tablespoon of the reserved bacon and onion heaped in the center of the bowl.

Makes 4 servings

Yankee Cajun Gumbo

I call this Yankee Cajun because I felt a little self-conscious about being an Ohio girl making gumbo in Louisiana. They are pretty passionate about it, but I did get an approving nod from a native when I asked her to try my version. Another thing I learned is that you can use just about any meat and seafood you have on hand and combinations of the two are common. Just match the flavor of the stock to the protein you want to use. For example, you don't really want a seafood stock if you are only using the smoked sausage and turkey; however, it would be perfect if you're going to include crawfish. While white rice is the traditional accompaniment, couscous is equally tasty.

2 Tablespoons unsalted butter
2 Tablespoons olive oil
1 yellow onion, finely chopped
½ green bell pepper, finely chopped
½ red bell pepper, finely chopped
2 ribs celery, finely chopped
3 Tablespoons no-salt Cajun seasoning blend, divided
¼ cup all-purpose flour
3 cups stock-choice depending on meats/seafood used
½ pound fresh okra, ends trimmed without cutting into pod
1 can (15 ounces) diced tomatoes in juice
½ pound smoked sausage, chopped
½ pound bite-sized pieces of meat, poultry or seafood (consider shrimp, crawfish, crab, pork, turkey, chicken or duck), meats should be cooked, seafood can be raw
3 cups hot cooked white rice, for serving
Filé powder, for serving
Tabasco sauce, for serving

In a heavy 3-quart saucepan over medium-high heat, melt the butter with the olive oil. Add the onion, green and red peppers and celery along with 1 Tablespoon of the Cajun seasonings.

SAVORY ASIDE

Say fee-lay.

Filé powder, sometimes called gumbo filé, will thicken a gumbo and add a distinctive kick of flavor. It is a simple ingredient made from the ground leaves of the sassafras tree. With a homey taste that is similar to thyme combined with savory, ground sassafras will lend a unique flavor to stews, sauces and other hearty dishes. It also serves as a thickening agent, but should only be stirred in at the end of cooking. If allowed to boil, filé powder will cause a liquid to become stringy and unappetizing.

Cook, stirring regularly, about 5 minutes or until the vegetables just begin to brown. Sprinkle in the flour; continue cooking, stirring constantly about 5 minutes more or until the mixture has taken on a deep golden brown. Slowly whisk in the stock, scraping the bottom of the pan and mixing well to avoid lumps. Bring to a boil, reduce heat to medium or enough to maintain a gentle boil and allow to simmer until it thickens, another 5 minutes or so. Reduce the heat to medium-low, stir in the okra, tomatoes, smoked sausage and remaining 2 Tablespoons of Cajun seasonings. Simmer for 10-15 minutes or until the okra is tender. Stir in the meat or seafood you have chosen and simmer until heated or cooked through. Taste and adjust for salt as necessary

To serve: Mound about ½ cup rice in the center of a shallow soup bowl. Ladle 1½ cups gumbo over the rice and sprinkle with filé powder, if desired. Pass the Tabasco at the table.

Makes 6 servings

Meatball Minestrone

Miniature meatballs make this a meal in a bowl. It is one of my favorite recipes of all time, especially with the added touch of velvety olive oil at the end. If you are counting on leftovers, you may want to keep the pasta on the side, adding handfuls to each bowl as it is served, because the pasta will become saturated and soggy in storage.

---

2 Tablespoons unsalted butter
2 Tablespoons olive oil
1 large yellow onion, chopped
1 red bell pepper, chopped
1 green bell pepper, chopped
1 large carrot, peeled and sliced
2 ribs celery, sliced
1 teaspoon dried oregano, divided
½ teaspoon dried basil, divided
½ teaspoon dried thyme, divided
¼ teaspoon dried marjoram, divided
2 cloves garlic, minced
1 cup chopped cabbage, green, Savoy or Napa
1 can (15 ounces) diced tomatoes in juice
1 can (15 ounces) kidney beans, drained
1 can (15 ounces) garbanzo beans, rinsed and drained
4 cups beef broth
½ teaspoon salt
¼ teaspoon freshly milled black pepper
1 pound Mini Meatballs, cooked (page 103)
1 large zucchini, cut into half moons
2 cups cooked small shell pasta, or other small pasta shape
¾ cup fresh minced herb mix such as basil, oregano, parsley, thyme and marjoram
Extra virgin olive oil, for serving
Freshly grated Parmesan cheese, for serving

Melt the butter with the olive oil in a soup kettle over medium-high heat. Stir in the onion, bell peppers, carrots, celery and half the dried herbs; cook, stirring regularly, for about 5 minutes. Add the garlic and cabbage; stir and cook 3 minutes more. Stir in the tomatoes, kidney beans, garbanzo

---

beans, remaining dried herbs, beef broth and 1 cup of water. Bring to a boil. Reduce the heat and simmer for about 10 minutes or longer to develop flavors.

About 15 minutes before serving, add the salt and pepper with the meatballs and zucchini. About 5 minutes before serving, add the pasta and fresh herbs. Taste for seasonings; adjust if necessary.

To serve, ladle into pasta bowls, drizzle with olive oil and top with a hefty pinch of cheese.

Makes 8 servings

Hungarian-Style Goulash

I've done an informal survey and it seems most moms made a dish called "goulash" but, every version is different. My mom's involved ground beef, macaroni and tomatoes. On a trip to Budapest I learned that true goulash is more of a soup and is often served as a starter rather than an entrée. We also enjoyed it made with chicken and goose.

---

2 Tablespoons vegetable oil
1 medium onion, finely chopped
8 ounces top sirloin beef, or other tender cut, cut into small cubes
2 Tablespoons Hungarian paprika
2 cups beef stock
1 cup chicken stock
2 medium baking potatoes, peeled and cubed ½-inch
1 large carrot, peeled and cubed ½-inch
1 bay leaf

Heat the oil in a 3-quart saucepan over medium-high heat. Add the onion and cook, stirring regularly, until softened and beginning to brown, about five minutes. Reduce heat to medium.

Meanwhile, toss the beef cubes with the paprika on a paper towel until the beef is well coated. Add to the pan with the onions after the heat has been reduced. Stir the beef with the onions. Cook for about 7 minutes, stirring and scraping the bottom of the pan while watching carefully so that the paprika doesn't burn. Remove the pan from the heat if you feel like it's getting away from you. Add the beef and chicken stocks along with ½ cup water, the potatoes, the carrots and the bay leaf. Bring to a boil. Reduce heat to a simmer. Cook for about 45 minutes, stirring occasionally, until the potatoes begin to break down and thicken the soup.

Makes 4 cups

Rosemary-Rye Dinner Scones, page 63

Breads: With breakfast, lunch or dinner

Different cooks look at baking bread in a variety of ways. For some, the opportunity to plunge their hands into a batch of dough is bliss. For others, attempting to bake bread is akin to creating an ice sculpture—simply out of the question.

Through my years as a cook, I have had the good fortune to work in many kitchens that I enjoyed. One job I loved in particular was cooking for a group of geologists at a remote lodge in Idaho. It was the perfect excuse to make bread everyday. I turned out loaves and muffins, rolls and biscuits.

Even if you are leery of making bread, press on. The recipes in this chapter are straightforward. The majority of them are quick breads with exciting flavors worked in.

Two exceptions are the Salt and Pepper Rolls and the Spiral Shallot Bread. These two breads are variations on the basic yeasted white loaf. The only secret is to knead the dough for the entire ten minutes, working in only as much flour as needed to maintain a soft dough that doesn't stick to your hands or the work surface.

The salt and pepper topping in the recipe for the rolls is only a starting point. The stark combination of black and white is attractive and tasty but by no means your only option. Consider creating a mixture of seeds or even a single seed topping that balances your menu. Cumin and crushed coriander would be right for a dinner with a Latin flair. Dill seeds with sesame and poppy would prove perfect with a tomato-based vegetable soup.

Seeds of all kinds are common in bread baking. They stand up well in the heat of the oven while providing crunch and taste to the final product. Sprinkled on top of a loaf, the seeds toast as the bread bakes.

In the recipe for Almond Poppy Seed Muffins, the tiny blue-black seed takes center stage. These not-too-sweet muffins are rich in flavor from almond extract in the batter while sliced almonds on top are oven-toasted for a pleasing crunch.

Muffins may be the simplest of the quick breads. Like the basic bread recipe, they have only one secret. Don't overmix. By combining the wet ingredients and dry ingredients separately and then just barely blending them together, you get a moist and tender, cakelike muffin.

Don't relegate muffins just to breakfast. As you can see from the Seeded Rye Muffins and the Sausage and Sage Corn Muffins, these savory nuggets also have a place on the dinner table.

Like seeds, rosemary is sturdy enough to take the heat of the oven, so it is commonly used in breads like potato rolls or worked into focaccia. Here, we use it as a savory addition to scones.

Consider growing your own rosemary, if at all possible. The fresh leaves stripped from their woody stems and roughly chopped are always a better alternative than dried rosemary. The flavor just doesn't seem to be the same in the dried version and you often get unpalatable bits of twig.

Perhaps the most mistreated and misunderstood quick bread of all is the biscuit. It should not be a dense, lackluster little hunk of dough. A biscuit should be light as a feather with tender flakes. This requires an easy touch and fast, hot baking. Their lifespan is short; the sooner they are eaten after emerging from the oven, the better.

Witness the technique in the recipe for Cinnamon Biscuits. Skip the last step and leave them plain if you just want a basic bread accompaniment. Adding the cinnamon sugar makes breakfast biscuits that bring fragrance and a splash of color to the table.

For most of my life we had two choices for cinnamon: ground or sticks, and they weren't even true cinnamon but cassia. These days we have an array of choices from around the world. If you are a real fan of the flavor you might want to experiment with the different varieties to see which you prefer. Consider grinding your own from cinnamon bits or sticks to unleash the freshest taste.

Biscuits are the basis for the fragrant and impressive-looking Pesto Pinwheels. With their Italian bent, these dinner biscuits are an unusual alternative to breadsticks or garlic toast. Any type of pesto will work, but I especially like to use the Cooking School Pesto for its tiny flecks of red, a result of the added tomatoes.

Yet another type of quick bread is the scone, tortured perhaps even more than the biscuit by poor preparation and being served long past its prime. One bite of a Cardamom Pecan Scone fresh from the oven will tell you all you need to know about how a scone should taste.

These scones' musky citrus flavor with hints of menthol may surprise those who aren't familiar with cardamom. This highly scented spice has a variety of typical uses that vary depending

SAVORY ASIDE

Baking Tips.

Keep a can of cooking oil spray on hand. In addition to coating pans, you can use it to oil bowls for rising bread and use on your hands and rolling pin to keep dough from sticking. Most ovens bake unevenly. You get better results if you turn a baking pan around halfway through the cooking time. Cooling racks really do make a difference. Circulating air keeps the underside of cookies and crackers crisp. On a rack, breads and muffins cool quickly, preventing internal heat buildup that may create an overbaked texture. Heighten the flavor of nuts and seeds by toasting them in a dry skillet over medium-high heat until fragrant and lightly browned. Allow them to cool before adding to recipes.

on region. Cardamom flavors coffee in Saudi Arabia, baked goods in Sweden and ground meat in Norway. It is a common ingredient in Eastern Indian curries.

Look for the whole green pods or seeds rather than buying cardamom in ground form as it loses flavor quickly after grinding. The pods should be split open so that you can remove the seeds, then crush them just before using.

The Shallot Spiral Bread is the star of this chapter. In the original recipe, a savory concoction of slivered shallots caramelized with thyme leaves is rolled into the loaf for an dazzling presentation. If it seems like too much work to make a roll, you can always work the filling into the dough.

So you see, serving fresh bread with a meal need not be complicated or time consuming. Think of it as a necessary part of a flavorful meal. Once you have worked your way through the breads in this chapter you will be poised to incorporate your own ideas into seasoning muffins, biscuits and loaves.

Almond Poppy Seed Muffins

You decide how sweet you want these muffins to be. With ½ cup sugar you get a tasty muffin that's not too sweet—good for the dinner table. Use a full cup of sugar if you're looking for a bakery-style treat.

¼ cup poppy seeds
2 cups all-purpose flour
½ cup to 1 cup sugar, depending on taste
1 teaspoon baking powder
½ teaspoon salt
¼ teaspoon baking soda
1 large egg
1½ cups buttermilk
1 teaspoon almond extract
5 Tablespoons unsalted butter, melted
3 Tablespoons sliced almonds

Toast the poppy seeds by placing them in a small dry skillet over medium-high heat and stirring constantly until fragrant, 2-3 minutes. Transfer to a small plate to cool.

Preheat the oven to 400 degrees. Butter a standard 12-cup muffin tin, or coat it with non-stick cooking spray.

Combine the flour, sugar, baking powder, salt, baking soda and the toasted poppy seeds in a large bowl. In a smaller bowl or measuring cup, mix the buttermilk with the egg and almond extract; add to the dry ingredients along with the melted butter. Stir just until barely mixed. Batter will be thick and lumpy.

Divide the batter between the muffin cups, filling almost full. Lightly press the sliced almonds over the top of the muffins. Bake for 15 minutes, or until the tops are dry and lightly browned. Cool slightly before removing the muffins from the tin and cool on a rack or serve immediately.

Makes 1 dozen

Sage and Sausage Corn Muffins

The perfect addition to a hearty dinner, these muffins are a snap to prepare. Assemble all the other ingredients while the sausage cooks. I like to use breakfast links for this recipe because they are usually packaged in "pre-measured" one ounce portions.

---

6 ounces breakfast sausage, casings removed (if necessary)
1 cup all-purpose flour
½ cup stone-ground yellow cornmeal
1 Tablespoon minced fresh sage
2 teaspoons sugar
1½ teaspoons baking powder
½ teaspoon baking soda
½ teaspoon salt
1 cup buttermilk
2 large eggs
5 Tablespoons unsalted butter, melted

Crumble the sausage into a small skillet over medium heat. Fry the sausage, breaking up the larger clumps, until crisp. Drain and chop into fine bits. Set aside.

Preheat the oven to 400 degrees. Butter a standard 12-cup muffin tin, or coat it with non-stick spray.

Combine the flour, cornmeal, sage, sugar, baking powder, baking soda and salt in a large bowl. In a smaller bowl or measuring cup, mix the buttermilk and eggs; add to the dry ingredients along with the melted butter and reserved sausage. Stir until barely mixed. Batter will be thick and lumpy.

SAVORY ASIDE

Mini Munchies.

My mini-muffin tin may be the most used piece of bakeware in the kitchen. With 24 cups, it accommodates any muffin recipe that calls for a standard 12-cup tin. You'll have to reduce the baking time by about five minutes in most cases. Mini-muffins are ideal for potlucks or other gatherings where large amounts of food are provided. Muffins freeze well. I like to pack them in small parcels of two large or six minis. Press out as much air as possible from the bag and then pack all the bags together in a larger freezer bag. Remove as many as you need for a snack or to accompany a meal and thaw at room temperature. If you are in a hurry, defrost the muffins in the bag for about 45 seconds in the microwave before wrapping in a napkin or paper towel (to absorb any moisture) and heat at medium low for another 45 seconds

Divide the batter among the muffin cups, using about ¼ cup for each muffin. Bake for 12 to 15 minutes, or until the tops are dry and lightly browned. Cool slightly before removing the muffins from the tin. Serve warm. Refrigerate any extras.

Makes 1 dozen

or so. Those little bags of muffins make a great grab-and-go breakfast or an impromptu hostess gift when you're invited for tea.

Seeded Rye Muffins

These little gems are just the bread to serve with a hearty bowl of soup. I like to bake them in the mini-muffin pan and then sock away any extras in the freezer to round out lunch on another day. They do take well to a spot of jam, if you would like them on the breakfast table.

---

1 cup whole wheat pastry flour
1 cup rye flour
1 teaspoon salt
1 teaspoon baking powder
½ teaspoon baking soda
1 teaspoon black sesame seeds
1 teaspoon white sesame seeds
½ teaspoon dill seeds
½ teaspoon caraway seeds
¼ teaspoon celery seeds
1 cup buttermilk
1 large egg
$^1/_3$ cup vegetable oil
2 Tablespoons honey

Preheat oven to 400 degrees. Butter a standard 12-cup muffin tin, or coat it with non-stick spray.

Combine the flours with the salt, baking powder, baking soda and seeds in a large bowl. Combine the buttermilk, egg, oil and honey in a medium bowl; stir into the flour mixture, just until well moistened.

Spoon the batter into the prepared muffin tin, filling each cup a little more than halfway. Bake about 15 minutes, rotating pan halfway through, or until tops spring back when touched. Remove from oven, cool slightly; transfer to a wire rack to cool completely or serve them right away.

Makes 1 dozen

Caraway Quick Bread

Soft and savory, this round loaf is easy to mix up and bakes while you prepare the rest of the meal. It is a natural accompaniment to the Split Pea Stew on page 44. Whole wheat pastry flour creates a whole grain bread that isn't too dense. It is especially good served warm. To reheat later, wrap a wedge loosely in a paper towel and microwave on half heat for 20 to 30 seconds.

---

1 cup whole wheat pastry flour
1 cup rye flour
2 teaspoons baking powder
½ teaspoon baking soda
½ teaspoon salt
1 teaspoon caraway seeds
2 large eggs
¾ cup buttermilk
¼ cup honey
4 Tablespoons (½ stick) unsalted butter, melted

Preheat the oven to 350 degrees. Butter an 8-inch round cake pan, or coat it with non-stick spray.

Combine the flours with the baking powder, baking soda, salt and caraway seeds in a medium mixing bowl. In a small bowl, whisk together the eggs, buttermilk and honey. Add to the flour mixture along with the melted butter. Stir until just blended. Pour into the prepared pan.

Bake 40 to 45 minutes, or until the top springs back when touched lightly. Transfer to a wire rack to cool slightly. Serve warm.

Makes 8 pieces

Cinnamon Biscuits

Kids will love these fragrant treats. Warm from the oven, the biscuits are soft while the cinnamon sugar bakes up to give a sweet crunch. It wouldn't be unthinkable to use these as a base for strawberry shortcakes, either.

---

2 Tablespoons sugar
1 teaspoon ground cinnamon
1 cup all-purpose flour
1 cup whole wheat pastry flour
1 Tablespoon baking powder
½ teaspoon salt
5 Tablespoons cold unsalted butter, sliced
1 cup plus 2 Tablespoons milk, divided

Preheat the oven to 400 degrees. Combine the sugar and cinnamon in a small bowl; set aside.

Combine the flours, baking powder and salt in a medium mixing bowl. Cut the sliced butter into flour mixture using a fork or pastry blender until the mixture resembles coarse crumbs. Gently stir in 1 cup of the milk just until a soft dough is formed.

Turn the dough out onto floured wax paper and knead lightly 6 or 8 times. Gather into a circle about ¾-inch thick. Use a floured cookie cutter or juice glass to cut circles of dough. To avoid waste, gather any uncut bits of dough and knead together to make a few more biscuits in the same manner.

Place the remaining 2 Tablespoons of milk in a small bowl. Dip the top of each biscuit into the milk, let any excess drip off and then dip into the cinnamon sugar, twisting just a bit in the sugar to coat well. Place on a greased cookie sheet, sugared side up.

SAVORY ASIDE

Bark makes a good bite.

Like so many of the great spices, cinnamon and cassia are harvested from evergreen trees, but in this case, it is not the fruit or seed that becomes the spice but the trunk. A special knife is used to cut strips of bark. The outer, cork-like layer of the bark is scraped off and the strips are left to dry. As they dry, they curl into the "quills" we know as cinnamon sticks. The finest cinnamon comes from Sri Lanka, once known as Ceylon; the finest cassia, from Saigon. When ground, true cinnamon takes on a tan color and cassia becomes the familiar reddish brown powder.

Bake for about 12 minutes, or until the bottoms are golden brown. Transfer to a wire rack to cool slightly. Serve warm.

Makes 12-15

Pesto Pinwheels

Shortening isn't used much these days but I keep it on hand just for biscuits. Look for the new varieties that contain no trans-fats. The pesto will make a very thin layer on the dough; it's just right when rolled, however, so don't be tempted to add more. Get the roll as tightly wound as you can for the most attractive presentation.

1$^1/_3$ cups all-purpose flour
2 teaspoons baking powder
¾ teaspoon salt
¼ teaspoon baking soda
4 Tablespoons shortening
$^2/_3$ cup buttermilk
¼ cup prepared pesto

Preheat the oven to 400 degrees.

In a small mixing bowl, combine the flour, baking powder, salt and baking soda. Use a fork to work in the shortening until no large lumps remain. Gently stir in the buttermilk just until the dough is moistened.

Turn out onto a floured sheet of waxed paper and knead a few times. Using a light touch with a rolling pin, flatten the dough into an even 14x10-inch rectangle. Spread the pesto evenly over the dough.

Beginning at one long end, use the waxed paper to nudge the dough into a tight roll. A bench scraper is helpful if the dough sticks to the paper. Using a floured serrated knife, slice the roll into

1-inch pieces, pinching lightly to keep them round. Transfer to an ungreased baking sheet, one cut side down, spacing the pinwheels about 1½-inches apart.

Bake for about 12 minutes, or until just beginning to brown on top. Serve warm.

Makes 15

Cardamom Pecan Scones

This method of grating frozen butter is an excellent way to achieve flaky scones; if you don't have time, simply use a fork to cut in cold butter that has been sliced into 12 pieces. Scones are best served the day they are baked.

1½ cups all-purpose flour
1½ cups whole wheat pastry flour
$^1/_3$ cup sugar, plus ¼ cup, divided
2½ teaspoons baking powder
¾ teaspoon salt
½ teaspoon baking soda
12 Tablespoons (1½ sticks) unsalted butter, frozen
1 cup plus 2 Tablespoons buttermilk
1 teaspoon freshly grated lemon zest, minced
4 green cardamom pods, seeds removed and crushed (about ¼ teaspoon)
$^2/_3$ cup chopped toasted pecans
1 egg white mixed with 1 teaspoon water

Preheat oven to 425 degrees.

Combine the flours, the $^1/_3$ cup sugar, baking powder, salt and baking soda in a mixing bowl. Use the large holes of a box grater to grate in the butter. Toss with a fork until all of the butter is coated with flour and the mixture resembles lumpy coarse crumbs. Add the buttermilk, lemon zest, cardamom and pecans; mix gently with the fork. The dough should be barely moist and won't come together completely until the next step.

Turn the dough onto a lightly floured board (or waxed paper), gather and knead very briefly, just until it comes together. Take care not to work too much extra flour into it. Divide the dough in half.

Form each half into a ½-inch thick circle and cut into 6 wedges. Place on an ungreased baking sheet, spaced slightly apart, brush the tops with the egg wash and sprinkle generously with the ¼ cup sugar.

Bake for 12 to 15 minutes, or until golden. Transfer to a wire rack to cool slightly. Serve warm.

Makes 1 dozen

Rosemary-Rye Dinner Scones

Cookbook authors often say their recipes are like children so they can't choose a favorite. Don't tell the other recipes, but as I write, this is my current favorite. These savory scones are bursting with flavors and have a texture that is so pleasing. They also make a wonderful cocktail snack when made in miniature. Just prepare the recipe as given and cut each large scone into quarters. Oddly enough, they take about the same amount of time to bake as full-size scones.

1½ cups all-purpose flour
1½ cups rye flour
2½ teaspoons baking powder
¾ teaspoon salt
½ teaspoon baking soda
12 Tablespoons (1½ sticks) unsalted butter, frozen
1 Tablespoon minced fresh rosemary
1¼ cups buttermilk
1 egg white mixed with 1 teaspoon water
2 teaspoons kosher salt

Preheat oven to 425 degrees.

Combine the flours, baking powder, salt and baking soda in a mixing bowl. Use the large holes of a box grater to grate in the butter. Toss with a fork until all of the butter is coated with flour and the mixture resembles lumpy coarse crumbs. Add the rosemary, toss to mix. Add the buttermilk; mix gently with the fork. The dough should be barely moist and won't come completely together until the next step.

Turn the dough onto a lightly floured board (or waxed paper), gather and knead very briefly, just until it comes together. Take care not to work too much extra flour into it. Divide the dough in half.

Form each half into a 7x7-inch square and cut into 9 squares. Place on an ungreased baking sheet, spaced slightly apart, brush the tops with the egg wash and sprinkle generously with the kosher salt.

Bake for 12 to 15 minutes, or until golden. Transfer to a wire rack to cool slightly. Serve warm.

Makes 18

Salt and Pepper Rolls

These unusual rolls are dense and reminiscent of soft pretzels. They are excellent with soup or serve them with a sturdy sandwich spread like Old-Fashioned Ham Salad (page 174) or Basic Chicken Salad (page 175) for an informal lunch or heavier appetizer.

2½ teaspoons active dry yeast
¼ cup water (110 degrees)
½ cup warm milk (110 degrees—about 25 seconds on high microwave)
1 Tablespoon unsalted butter, softened
2 teaspoons honey
1 teaspoon salt
2¼ cups bread flour
Non-stick spray
1 egg white, beaten

1 teaspoon coarse or flaked sea salt
½ teaspoon cracked black pepper

Sprinkle the yeast over the water in a medium bowl, stir to moisten; allow to sit for 5 minutes or until creamy. Add the milk, butter, honey, salt and 1 cup of the flour. Mix well to make a smooth batter, using the back of the spoon to work in the butter. Work in another 1 cup of the flour until the dough is moistened (at this point, it will be quite soft).

Sprinkle remaining ¼ cup of flour onto a work surface and turn out the dough from the bowl. Knead for 10 minutes, working in as little of the flour as needed to keep it from sticking. Tacky is okay but it shouldn't leave bits of dough on your work surface or hands. Coat the mixing bowl with cooking oil spray. Transfer the dough to the bowl and spray the top; cover with plastic wrap and let rise until doubled, about 45 minutes.

Move the dough back to the floured work surface and press into an 8x6-inch rectangle. Cut into 12 2x2-inch equal pieces; space them out evenly on an oiled baking sheet. Cover and let rest for another 45 minutes.

Meanwhile, preheat the oven to 400 degrees.

Just before baking, brush each roll lightly with the beaten egg white. Combine the salt and pepper and sprinkle onto the top of each roll.

Bake 12 to 15 minutes, or until lightly browned. Transfer to a wire rack to cool slightly. Serve warm.

Makes 1 dozen

Shallot Spiral Bread

Look for shallots alongside other onions and garlic at the market. They have a shorter shelf life than some of their cousins, but that's okay. Once you start using shallots, you will find it is hard to keep them on hand. If you don't want to go to the trouble of making the spiral, work the shallot mixture into the dough during the last five minutes of kneading. This is messy and slippery (and sort of fun) at first, but it works.

---

1 Tablespoon unsalted butter
1 Tablespoon olive oil
1 teaspoon dried thyme
1½ cups thinly sliced shallots (5-10, depending on size)
Salt and freshly milled black pepper, to taste
1 cup warm water
2½ teaspoons active dry yeast
1 Tablespoon sugar
3 cups all-purpose flour, approximately
2 Tablespoons unsalted butter, at room temperature
1 teaspoon salt
Non-stick spray
1 egg white, beaten
Poppy seeds

In a medium skillet, melt the butter with the olive oil over medium heat. Add the thyme, then the shallots, mixing well to coat with the butter mixture. Cook slowly until very soft, about 15 minutes, stirring frequently so that the shallots don't brown too much. Remove from heat, stir in salt and pepper and set aside.

Pour the warm water into a large mixing bowl. Sprinkle with the yeast and the sugar; stir and allow to stand for 5 minutes. Mix in 1 cup of the flour along with the butter and salt. Stir until well blended, breaking up the butter as needed. Add another 1½ cups of the flour. Stir until the dough "cleans the bowl." Turn it out onto a lightly floured board or counter top. Knead for 10 minutes, adding as little flour as possible. Ideally, after 5 minutes you will have a ball of dough that is slightly tacky but not sticky and will not need to have flour on your board.

Shake out any excess flour from the mixing bowl and coat with the non-stick spray. Form the dough into a ball, place in the bowl and lightly coat the top with the spray. Cover loosely with plastic wrap. Allow the dough to rise in a warm place until doubled in size, about 45 minutes.

Punch the dough down and turn it out onto a lightly floured surface. Use a rolling pin to form a rectangle that measures 9x22-inches. Spread the shallot mixture in a thin, even layer over the dough. Beginning at one long end, roll the dough into a tight loaf shape. Pat the ends in and fit it into a greased loaf pan, seam side down. Cover loosely with plastic wrap and allow to rise again until it has risen over the top of the pan, 30 to 45 minutes. Meanwhile, preheat the oven to 375 degrees.

Before transferring the loaf to the oven, brush the beaten egg white over the top and sprinkle with poppy seeds. Bake for 20 to 25 minutes, until the top is browned and the bread has reached an internal temperature of 190 degrees on an instant read thermometer.

Makes 1 loaf

Chickpea Flatbread

Chickpea, or garbanzo bean, flour is available at natural foods stores. It adds a toothsome quality to this frybread and stands up to bold toppings. The flour makes a savory coating for the Curry-Garbanzo variation of Tropical Fish, too (page 113). This flatbread is the base for the Tomato-Za'atar Appetizers on page 16.

---

1 cup chickpea flour
1 cup all-purpose flour
2 teaspoons baking powder
1 teaspoon salt
2 Tablespoons shortening
$^2/_3$ cup warm water
Peanut oil for frying

Combine the flours with the baking powder and salt in a medium mixing bowl. Use a fork to work the shortening into the dry ingredients until the mixture resembles fine crumbs. Add the water slowly to form a soft, somewhat crumbly, dough. Knead for a minute or two to bring it together into a smooth mass. Form the dough into a ball. Cover with plastic wrap and allow the dough to rest in the refrigerator for 30 minutes.

In a cooking pot suitable to deep frying, heat a half-inch of oil over medium-high heat until a tiny piece of dough sizzles and floats when dropped in.

Meanwhile, on a lightly floured surface, roll half of the dough (for ease in handling, keep remaining half covered) to $^1/_8$-inch thick. Use a pizza-cutter to cut the dough into approximately 3x5-inch rectangles. Brush off excess flour. Repeat with remaining half of dough.

Working with 3 or 4 rectangles at a time, depending on size of pan, carefully slide the dough into the hot oil. Fry until puffed and golden on one side then turn to cook other side, about three minutes altogether. Use a slotted spoon to remove the bread to paper towels for draining. Continue the process until all the dough is cooked.

Serve warm or at room temperature. These are best the day they are made.

Makes about 24

Sesame Wheat Crackers

I'm always trying to avoid trans-fats but it seems especially difficult when it comes to crackers. This recipe provides a great alterative to store-bought. These are excellent with any sort of cheese. Tahini, a common ingredient in hummus, is a prepared paste of sesame seeds. Look for it and gar-banzo bean flour in the natural foods section of your supermarket. If you happen to have two 9x11-inch pans, by all means bake all of the crackers at the same time.

---

1 cup whole wheat pastry flour
½ cup garbanzo bean flour
½ teaspoon salt
¼ teaspoon baking powder
2 teaspoons white sesame seeds
2 teaspoons black sesame seeds (or use all white seeds)
½ cup tahini
½ cup milk
2 Tablespoons vegetable oil
Non-stick cooking spray

Preheat the oven to 350 degrees.

Combine the flours, salt, baking powder and seeds in a mixing bowl; stir well. With a fork, mix in the tahini until the mixture resembles coarse crumbs. Add the milk and oil; stir until the dry in-gredients are moistened.

Divide the dough in half; wrap one half in plastic while you work with the other. Lightly coat a 9x11-inch cookie sheet, your hands and a rolling pin with the cooking spray. Roll out half of the dough into a thin, even layer that fills the sheet (if your rolling pin is too big, a wine bottle will work). Score the dough by making 6 lengthwise cuts and 8 crosswise cuts that don't go all the way through. Perforate the entire surface with a fork, 3 jabs to a cracker.

Bake for 15-20 minutes, rotating the pan halfway through cooking, or until the crackers are stiff and the edges are deep brown. The crackers will crisp up as they cool. Remove from pan; cool com-pletely on a wire rack. Break along score lines into individual crackers. Repeat process with other half of dough. Store in an airtight container.

Makes about 10 dozen

Polenta Stacks, page 82

Breakfast: More than just a morning meal

For most of us in this grab-and-go world, the big breakfast is a luxury. And when we can afford the time to indulge in a morning feast, we worry about fat and calories and cholesterol. Although a few of these recipes fit that bill, the majority might be considered healthy compromises. "They" say eggs are okay now, and with all of the low-fat dairy alternatives available today, maybe breakfast can make a comeback.

Herbs and spices are not often associated with breakfast but there is plenty of room for them, especially if healthy food is a priority. They help add flavor without more fat or salt. In the case of chiles and onions, we also get the benefit of a boost of Vitamin C.

All the vegetables including chiles and garlic in the recipe for Daniel's Easter Eggs are a great example. What seems like a major morning indulgence actually has very little fat, especially if the eggs are fried in a non-stick skillet.

Chiles have a place in the herb garden during those long summer days. They are an attractive plant that requires little attention. The varieties are endless if you look beyond the jalapeno. Consider Hungarian, poblano, or even habaneros if you can take the heat.

Canned hominy, a sort of puffed up corn, is the main ingredient in The Best Breakfast Yet, but the bright bite of chiles is the star. This is a hearty meal best saved for a morning when you can put your feet up and read the newspaper after you have eaten.

Corn pops up again in the recipe for Polenta Stacks. Some folks say polenta is nothing more than fancy grits, and they would be right. Both are made from coarsely ground corn, offering us a pleasant, almost nutty flavor and plenty of texture. In the stacks, polenta serves both as the stage for a poached egg and is cubed for a colorful garnish. Quick Fresh Salsa makes the flavors sing.

I do love all members of the onion family. Like chiles, they are not out of place in your herb garden. Chives are a natural, but garlic and shallots are fun to try as well. Shallots have a sort of garlicky onion flavor. They are a major part of the filling for the Winter Quiche and serve as a savory accent for fresh or dried herbs.

Grains are a stick-to-your ribs option for breakfast that never fails to satisfy. Bland on their own, they can become outstanding with the addition of spices. Cinnamon and a hint of orange make unusual grains seem familiar in the Kasha, Quinoa and Couscous Cereal.

The warm taste of mace feels like a motherly hug in the Fruit 'n Barley Flakes, a dish that is as easy to serve as cereal from a box. Barley flakes need only their equal amount of boiling water plus ten minutes, replacing the long cooking time needed for pearled barley but are still full of nutrition.

Fruit in some form or another is a must-have for breakfast in my book. I often whirl up some berries or a banana with tofu, soy milk and honey for something quick.

Take advantage of the summer harvest by freezing berries. It's easy to do. Spread a single layer of berries on a paper-lined baking sheet and freeze them. Once frozen, transfer them to a heavy-duty plastic bag, squeeze out as much air as possible, and fresh tasting berries are at your fingertips all year long. Take the caps off of strawberries before freezing, and be sure to pit cherries if you want to preserve those in the same way.

As we have learned, mom was right when she said, "Breakfast is the most important meal of the day." Now we know we have plenty of options other than just bacon and eggs. Make your way through these recipes each morning, develop a few of your own variations and the most important meal will never be the most boring meal of the day.

Nutty Granola

Once you have made your own granola you will forget all about those high-calorie boxed brands. I like to stir this into yogurt, but you might also consider it as a topping for a simple, single-serve breakfast fruit crisp. Heat some frozen fruit in a bowl in the microwave, top with the granola and, poof, you've got a makeshift crisp.

2½ cups oatmeal, not instant
¾ cup chopped mixed nuts
½ cup wheat germ
¼ cup unsweetened shredded coconut
¼ cup sunflower seeds
¼ cup sesame seeds
½ cup frozen apple juice concentrate
¼ cup honey
¼ cup vegetable oil
1 Tablespoon vanilla extract

Preheat the oven to 350 degrees.

Combine the oatmeal, nuts, wheat germ, coconut and seeds in a large bowl.

Stir the apple juice concentrate, honey and oil together in a small saucepan. Bring to a boil over medium-high heat. Remove from heat; stir in vanilla. Pour this liquid over the oat mixture in the bowl and mix well.

Spread the granola evenly on a large baking sheet with a rim. Bake for about 30 minutes, stirring every 5 minutes with a wide spatula, until the granola takes on a deep caramel color. The toasting time will vary by the size of the pan used and granola can burn quickly. Each time you stir, listen for signs that it is becoming crisp—as it begins to make more sound on the baking sheet, it is getting closer. It will crisp up further as it cools.

Store in an airtight container. Granola can be frozen for up to three months.

Makes about 3½ cups

Gingered Peaches

Think of these silky peaches as a breakfast sauce. They are a perfect alternative to maple syrup on pancakes or waffles, but the snappy flavors would also be a welcome topping for a bowl of oatmeal (not to mention ice cream). Thawed frozen peaches work well here and save the time of peeling.

5 Tablespoons unsalted butter
1½ teaspoons ground ginger
3 cups peeled and sliced peaches
$^1/_3$ cup packed brown sugar

Melt the butter in a skillet over medium heat. Add the ginger and stir for a minute before adding the peaches and brown sugar. Mix well; cook for about 5 minutes, or until the liquids become syrupy.

Makes 2 cups

Fruit 'n Barley Flakes

I learned about barley flakes from Mollie Katzen's *Sunlight Café* cookbook. They look like oats but have a savory flavor that makes a great stand-in for rice. Look for barley flakes in the natural food section of your supermarket or order online. This nourishing combination of fruits and grains is good hot or cold, with milk poured over it or not.

½ cup barley flakes
¼ teaspoon salt
1 Tablespoon unsalted butter
½ cup fresh blueberries
¾ cup chopped peaches or bananas
1 Tablespoon honey, or more to taste
¼ teaspoon ground mace

Bring ½ cup of water to a boil in a small saucepan. Stir in the barley flakes and salt, reduce heat to medium-low and cover. Cook for 5 minutes. Remove from heat and allow to stand, covered, for 5 minutes. Fluff with a fork; add the butter and fluff again. Stir in the honey and mace, then the fruits. Serve hot.

Makes 2 servings

Kasha, Quinoa and Couscous Cereal

Make one big batch of this nutritious grain mixture on the weekend and watch it save the day when you're pressed for time in the morning during the week. Using a variety of toppings keeps you from getting tired of the same old thing each day. My favorite combo is bananas and maple syrup, but equally satisfying is grated apple with brown sugar and a bit of butter.

$^2/_3$ cup kasha
½ cup quinoa, rinsed well
$2^1/_3$ cups water, plus ¼ cup
½ teaspoon salt
¼ teaspoon dried orange peel
¼ cup couscous
2 Tablespoons turbinado sugar
1 teaspoon ground cinnamon

Optional toppings: milk, sliced bananas, maple syrup, chopped nuts, coconut, blueberries, dried fruits, chopped fresh fruit (even chocolate chips!)

Combine the kasha, quinoa and $2^1/_3$ cups water, plus the salt and orange peel in a medium saucepan. Bring to a boil, reduce heat to low, cover and simmer for 15 minutes or until all the liquid is absorbed.

Meanwhile, heat the ¼ cup water in a 1 cup measure (or other small microwavable bowl) for 45 seconds. Stir in the couscous, cover and let stand for 5 minutes. Fluff with a fork.

SAVORY ASIDE

Muesli in a Minute.

Real muesli is not the granola-like mixture we often find on the cereal aisle. It is rich and creamy and studded with fruits and nuts. Make a quick version by adding grated apples, sunflower seeds, wheat germ, dried cranberries, coconut, plain yogurt and honey to the basic blend of Kasha, Quinoa and Couscous.

Once the kasha and quinoa have cooked, stir in the fluffed couscous, the sugar and the cinnamon.

Serve hot with your choice of toppings, using enough milk to achieve a consistency you enjoy.

Refrigerate leftovers for a few days or freeze in portions. To reheat, add a bit of milk and micro-wave on high for a minute or so, or warm slowly in a small saucepan over medium heat.

Makes 4 to 6 servings

Stuffed French Toast with Vanilla Strawberries

I wanted to go "upscale" with this seemingly decadent breakfast dish by using mascarpone in-stead of cream cheese, but when I tried it the mascarpone melted away and made the French toast soggy. This is one time when frozen strawberries simply won't do. You want the structure of fresh berries for the final presentation. Conversely, your bread shouldn't be too fresh or it will turn out soggy. If necessary, dry it out a bit with a brief blast in the toaster.

---

3 cups sliced fresh strawberries (about 20 large, with caps removed)
3 Tablespoons powdered sugar, plus 2 Tablespoons
4 teaspoons vanilla extract
¼ cup slightly softened cream cheese
2 large eggs
½ cup milk
4 slices hearty bread (not too fresh)

Toss the berries with the 3 Tablespoons of powdered sugar and the vanilla. Set aside, stirring gently every now and then, for at least 20 minutes but up to two hours.

Meanwhile, mix the remaining 2 Tablespoons sugar into the cream cheese; set aside.

When you are ready to prepare the French toast, place a large non-stick skillet or griddle over medium-high heat. Beat the eggs together in a shallow bowl and stir in the milk. Test the skillet to make sure it is hot enough by dripping a few drops of water from your fingertips: if the water sizzles and evaporates, it is ready. Coat the skillet lightly with non-stick cooking spray.

One slice at a time, dip only one side of the bread into the egg/milk batter and allow any excess to drip off. Place on the hot skillet coated side down. Repeat with the remaining three slices of bread. Cook until the batter is a deep golden brown, rearranging the bread as necessary to achieve an even color. Remove the skillet from the heat and transfer the bread to a board or other clean, dry spot with the uncoated sides down.

Now, spread half of the sweetened cream cheese on each of two of the cooked toasts. This might be a challenge as the cream cheese will melt slightly. Work slowly and try to get an even layer of the cheese. Top each with the remaining slices of bread toasted half down, so that you have a sandwich with two dry sides. Coat the skillet with more cooking spray and return to the heat. Dip each sandwich into the remaining egg/milk batter, coating both sides, and, allowing any excess to drip off. Cook in the same manner as before, rearranging as necessary for an even golden brown color, on both sides.

Once finished, plate the French toast, topping each with half of the strawberries and their accumulated juices.

Makes 2 servings

Butter Pecan Waffles

When I was a kid, my mom's favorite ice cream flavor was butter-pecan and I thought she was nuts. I much preferred the kind with bubble gum in it. Her combo works wonders when baked into a crispy breakfast treat. Waffles are another handy freezer item. Use a toaster to restore the crisp crust. I've been known to enjoy a waffle as an afternoon snack, but with a scoop of frozen yogurt and some chocolate sauce they would make a yummy dessert, too.

---

3 large eggs, separated
1½ cups buttermilk
½ cup (1 stick) unsalted butter, melted
2 teaspoons vanilla extract
1 cup all-purpose flour
1 cup whole wheat pastry flour
¾ cup finely chopped toasted pecans, plus ¼ cup roughly chopped, for garnish
2 Tablespoons granulated sugar
1 teaspoon salt
½ teaspoon baking soda
Scant ½ teaspoon ground mace

Whisk the egg yolks with the buttermilk, melted butter and vanilla until well blended. In a separate bowl, combine the flours, the ¾ cup pecans, sugar, salt, baking soda, and mace. Stir the dry ingredients into the egg and buttermilk mixture until just combined, some lumps are okay. Beat the egg whites to stiff peaks and fold into batter.

Bake the waffles according to your waffle iron manufacturer's guidelines.

To serve, sprinkle the remaining pecans on top. Pass warmed maple syrup and/or Gingered Peaches (page 75) at the table.

Makes 4 servings

Eggs Scrambled with Sprouts, Tomato and Cream Cheese

I will confess to keeping a bag of commercially prepared bacon bits in the fridge especially for this dish. Rather than the crunchy, artificial bacon bits often found on salad bars, look for a real bacon product or, of course, cook up a couple of strips.

---

8 large eggs
2 Tablespoons bacon bits
2 Tablespoons water
Salt, to taste
Freshly milled black pepper, to taste
¼ cup (2 ounces) cream cheese, cut into small chunks
1 large tomato, chopped
½ cup alfalfa, radish or broccoli sprouts

Heat a non-stick skillet coated with cooking spray over medium-heat.

Whisk the eggs with the bacon bits, water, salt and pepper. Pour into the hot skillet. Use a rubber spatula to keep the eggs moving as they cook. When the eggs have reached the degree of doneness you prefer, remove from heat and sprinkle with the cream cheese chunks, tomato and sprouts. Gently fold the eggs over the cream cheese so that it's mixed in but creamy spots of cheese remain.

Transfer to a warmed platter. Sprinkle with the black pepper and serve right away.

Makes 4 servings

SAVORY ASIDE

Sprout Your Own.

It is great fun to tend to your own sprouts and a sprouting kit makes it easy as can be. Daily rinsing, an absolute must, is your only time investment. Alfalfa is perhaps the most popular sprout, but a wide variety of sprouting seeds are available. Beyond grassy types like alfalfa and wheat, you will find beans such as garbanzo, adzuki and lentil, plus veggies like radish, onion and broccoli. Once you have a delectable package of home-grown spouts in your vegetable bin, you will find a million ways to use them. Garnish plates, add to salads or try my favorite, a bagel with cream cheese, sprouts and tomatoes.

Polenta Stacks

This pretty breakfast dish is as delightful to look at as it is to eat. Tubes of prepared polenta are readily available at well-stocked supermarkets. If you prefer to make your own, use a cookie cutter to form 2½- to 3-inch rounds. The recipe is for one serving, it multiplies out easily should you need more than that.

For each stack:
2 slices polenta, one ½-inch thick, the other ¼-inch thick
1 large egg, poached
¼ cup Quick Fresh Salsa (page 9) or bottled salsa, warmed
1 Tablespoon sour cream
¼ of an avocado, peeled and cubed
Cilantro leaves, for garnish, if desired

Coat a skillet with non-stick spray and set it over medium-high heat. Fry the polenta slices until golden brown on both sides, about 10 minutes total. Transfer the half-inch thick slice to a serving plate and cut the quarter-inch thick slice into cubes.

Top the polenta slice with the poached egg. Spoon salsa over the top and then add a dollop of sour cream. Scatter the avocado and cubed polenta around the base of the stack. Garnish with the cilantro, if using. Serve right away.

Makes 1 serving

Best Breakfast Yet

This creamy yet spicy combination is based on a recipe from Bert Greene's *Greene on Grains*. Around our house, we just call this the hominy stuff. It's one of my husband's favorite things to eat.

---

1 can (14 ounces) white hominy, drained and rinsed
¼ cup heavy cream (milk works in a pinch)
1 Tablespoon unsalted butter
2 Tablespoons canned diced green chiles
2 Tablespoons chopped pickled jalapenos
¼ cup (½ ounce) shredded Pepper-Jack cheese
Salt and freshly milled black pepper, to taste
4 poached eggs
2 slices buttered toast, cut in half diagonally
1 large tomato, cored and chopped

Puree the hominy with the heavy cream in a food processor fitted with the steel blade. Set aside.

Melt the butter in a small saucepan over medium heat. Stir in the creamed hominy, green chiles and jalapenos. Heat thoroughly, stirring often. Remove from heat and stir in the cheese, salt and pepper. Continue stirring until the cheese is melted.

To serve, divide evenly between two plates, leaving room on each plate for the toast and tomatoes. Make two indentions into the hominy on each plate and fill with the poached eggs. Sprinkle with more black pepper for garnish; add toast and tomatoes to each plate. Serve immediately.

Makes 2 servings

Daniel's Easter Eggs (Huevos Rancheros)

The first year we were in Mongolia we went to breakfast at a little cafe run by a Cuban fellow. It happened to be Easter Sunday and his special for that day was a wonderful plate of huevos. Such a treat! I plan to make it a tradition from now on.

---

6 8-inch flour tortillas, warmed
1½ cups warm Ranchero Sauce (recipe follows)
¾ cup (3 ounces) shredded cheese
1 batch Daniel's Mongolian salsa (recipe follows)
12 large eggs

Set a non-stick skillet over medium heat and ask everyone how they want their eggs. Cooking the eggs two at a time, you will need to work quickly in order to serve everyone a hot meal.

Set up an assembly line that begins with 6 dinner plates. Place 1 flour tortilla on each plate and build the dishes as you fry the eggs. On half of each tortilla spread ¼ cup of the ranchero sauce and sprinkle with 2 Tablespoons of the cheese. Top the cheese with 2 fried eggs and about ¼ cup of the Mongolian salsa. Fold over the unfilled half and top with a bit more of the Mongolian salsa to hold it closed. Serve right away.

Makes 6 servings

Ranchero Sauce

1 Tablespoon vegetable oil
1 medium yellow onion, chopped
1 poblano chile pepper, stemmed, seeded and chopped
2 garlic cloves, minced
½ teaspoon dried Mexican oregano
¼ teaspoon ground New Mexican chile
1 can (14 ounces) petite diced tomatoes
Salt, as needed

Heat the oil in a skillet over medium-high heat. Add the onion; cook, stirring regularly, for 3 minutes. Add the poblano chile and continue cooking 5 minutes more. Stir in the garlic, oregano and ground chile; cook and stir for 3 more minutes. Add the tomatoes and $1/_3$ cup of water. Bring to a boil. Reduce heat, simmer for 15 minutes. Taste for salt; adjust if needed.

Divide the cooked sauce in half. Puree one half in a food processor or with a hand-held blender; return to pot and stir into the remaining sauce. Serve warm, or cover, refrigerate, and use within 1 week.

Makes 2 cups

Daniel's Mongolian Salsa

1 Anaheim pepper, seeded and thinly sliced
1 jalapeno pepper, seeded, if desired, and thinly sliced
¼ of a red onion, thinly sliced
1 handful of minced cilantro
2 tomatoes, cored and chopped
Salt and freshly milled black pepper, to taste

Toss these ingredients together. Serve with Daniel's Easter Eggs or use as a garnish on other Mexican dishes.

Makes about 2 cups

SAVORY ASIDE

Dried but Fresh.

Light and heat are the enemies of your dried herbs and spices. To maintain the best quality, buy small amounts frequently, keep them in a closed cabinet that is away from the heat of the oven and cooktop. Remember, whole spices will keep longer, even years longer, than those you buy already ground.

Breakfast Tacos

You can't go wrong serving this hearty breakfast buffet when you need to feed a crowd. Make the morning easy on yourself by peeling and dicing the potatoes the night before. Keep them in a bowl of water to prevent browning.

---

1 roll (12 ounces) breakfast sausage
2 medium baking potatoes (about 1 pound), peeled and diced
1 yellow onion, minced
2 cloves garlic, minced
1 teaspoon ground cumin
½ teaspoon salt
$^1/_8$ teaspoon freshly milled black pepper
6 large eggs
1 dozen 8-inch flour tortillas, warmed
¾ cup (3 ounces) shredded cheddar cheese
½ cup sour cream
½ cup salsa

In a wide skillet over medium heat, cook the sausage until it's no longer pink, breaking up any large chunks. Drain, if necessary. Mix the potatoes, onion, garlic, cumin, salt and pepper with the sausage in the skillet. Cover; cook, stirring regularly, until the potatoes are cooked through, 10-15 minutes.

Just before serving, heat another skillet coated with non-stick spray over medium. Beat the eggs with 1 Tablespoon of water. When the skillet is hot, add the eggs; cook and stir to scramble them.

Serve the sausage-potato filling and eggs buffet-style with tortillas, cheese, sour cream and salsa, allowing each diner to fill their own tacos.

Makes 6 servings

Breakfast Fajitas

Eggs are fried hard and cut into strips for this fun morning take on traditional fajitas. I often have leftover brown rice, which was the inspiration here. You might consider stashing a couple of half-cup portions of rice in the freezer the next time you make it for dinner. If your tortillas are larger than six inches, just pile everything onto one for each serving.

---

2 teaspoons unsalted butter
2 teaspoons olive oil
½ cup thinly sliced yellow onion
½ cup thinly sliced bell pepper (combining red and green is attractive)
Salt and freshly milled black pepper, to taste
2 large eggs
4 6-inch flour tortillas, warmed
½ cup cooked brown rice, warm
Sour cream, salsa and guacamole, for serving

Melt the butter with the olive oil in a medium skillet over medium heat. Add the onion and bell pepper; cook, stirring frequently, until softened and beginning to brown, about 5 minutes or so. Season with salt and pepper to taste. Remove from skillet, set aside and keep warm.

Into the same skillet, crack each of the eggs, as if to fry, then break each yolk. Cook for about 90 seconds, carefully flip, season with salt and pepper, if desired, and continue cooking until set.

Working quickly, transfer the cooked eggs to a cutting board and slice them into strips. To assemble the fajitas, arrange 2 Tablespoons of the cooked rice down the center of each tortilla. Top each with an equal portion of the onion-bell pepper mixture and the egg strips. Fold each tortilla in half or roll up burrito-style. Serve immediately, passing the sour cream, salsa and guacamole at the table.

Makes 2 servings

Chile Relleno Quiche

Real chile rellenos can be time consuming to prepare. This quiche has similar flavors and is a snap to whip up. I often bake it the day before I want to serve it and reheat it in the oven for 20 minutes or so.

---

1 9-inch pie shell, unbaked
1 cup (4 ounces) shredded Pepper-Jack cheese
1 can (4 ounces) diced green chilies
4 large eggs
½ cup milk
½ teaspoon ground cumin
½ teaspoon salt
$^1/_8$ teaspoon freshly milled black pepper

Preheat oven to 400 degrees. Parbake the pie shell: Prick the entire surface, even the sides, with the tines of a fork. Line the shell with parchment paper and fill the cavity with dried beans or pie weights. Bake for 10 minutes. Set aside to cool. Reduce oven temperature to 375 degrees.

Place the pie shell on a baking sheet. Sprinkle the cheese evenly over bottom of pie shell. Spoon the green chilies over the cheese in an even layer. Whisk together the eggs, cream, cumin, salt and pepper; pour over the cheese and chilies.

Bake for about 40 minutes or until the center is set and the top is beginning to brown. Allow to sit for 10 minutes before slicing.

Makes 4 to 6 servings

Winter Quiche

I wanted to make a mixed herb quiche but the day I was set to bake, the herb garden was under a blanket of snow. A quick whirl of the spice rack offered inspiration in the form of a packet of herbes de Provence I had purchased on impulse a few months before. The classic French herb blend turned out to be a delicious seasoning for this ultra creamy quiche.

---

1 9-inch pie shell, unbaked
1 Tablespoon unsalted butter
1 Tablespoon olive oil
2 cups (about 7-8 medium) shallots, peeled, halved and thinly sliced
½ teaspoon salt, plus ¼ teaspoon
1 Tablespoon dried herbes de Provence
2 cups (about 6 ounces) shredded Fontina cheese
3 large eggs
1¼ cups half-and-half
$^1/_8$ teaspoon freshly milled black pepper

Preheat the oven to 400 degrees. Parbake the pie shell: Prick the entire surface, even the sides, with the tines of a fork. Line with parchment paper and fill the cavity with dried beans or pie weights and then bake in the preheated oven for 10 minutes. Set aside to cool while you prepare the filling. Turn off the oven for now.

In a wide skillet over medium-high heat, melt the butter with the olive oil. Add the shallots, sprinkle with the ½ teaspoon salt and toss well to coat with the butter and oil. Cook, stirring regularly, until the shallots are softened and beginning to brown, 5 to 10 minutes. Remove from the heat and stir in the herbes de Provence; allow to cool completely before proceeding.

Once the shallots have cooled, preheat the oven to 400 degrees again. Mix the cheese into the shallots and spread evenly over the parbaked pie shell.

Whisk the eggs in a medium mixing bowl. Add the half-and-half, the ¼ teaspoon salt and the pepper and whisk well to combine. Pour this mixture over the cheese and shallots.

Bake for about 30 minutes, or until the top is golden brown and the center is set. Allow to sit for 10 minutes before slicing.

Makes 4 to 6 servings

Herb Garden Quiche variation: Replace the herbes de Provence with ¼ cup of minced fresh herbs.

Asparagus Ham Roll-Ups

This is an attractive way to serve ham at the breakfast table while sneaking in a vegetable. Of course, you don't have tie up the bundles with the carrot and green onion strips, but it looks pretty and is easy to do once you get the hang of it.

---

12 asparagus spears
2 teaspoons olive oil
Kosher salt, to taste
Freshly milled black pepper, to taste
¼ cup mayonnaise
2 Tablespoons Dijon-style mustard
1 Tablespoon snipped chives
6 thin slices (about 8 ounces) smoked ham
6 thin strips each of carrot and green onion

Preheat the oven to 450 degrees.

Trim the tough blunt ends from the asparagus spears. Toss with olive oil and sprinkle with salt and pepper. Arrange the spears in a baking dish just large enough to hold them a single layer. Roast for 10 minutes, turn them and roast 5 minutes more. Remove from oven and reduce the temperature to 400 degrees.

Meanwhile, combine the mayonnaise, mustard and chives in a small bowl. Using a pastry brush, paint this mixture evenly over the slices of ham. (You may not use it all. Any extra makes a good sandwich spread.) Place 2 asparagus spears on the center of each slice of ham, pointing in opposite directions so the blossom ends just show at the edge and roll up each slice. Place the roll-ups seam side down on a parchment paper-lined baking sheet.

Bake for about 10 minutes, until hot but not browning. Twist together 1 carrot strip and one green onion strip and tie around the center of each roll-up. Serve hot.

Makes 6 servings

Braised Pork Chops with Creamy Mustard Sauce, page 105

Meats, Chicken and Fish: Mostly turf, some surf

Creating main dishes introduces opportunities to employ the entire arsenal of your spice cabinet. The wide assortment of recipes that follow highlights that theme.

You may notice that some seasonings come up again and again in different combinations. Thyme, garlic and parsley, in particular, will stand on their own or serve to enhance other flavors.

Thyme is a worthy plant to grow in the herb garden. In all but the coldest climates, this low-growing shrub is a constant provider. It is evergreen and will be one of the first herbs to show growth in the spring.

Oregano stars in Italian dishes and plays a not-so-minor part in many others. Consider investing in a jar of Mexican oregano in addition to the traditional Greek variety. Mexican oregano has a somewhat wild flavor that suits spicy dishes like chili or tacos.

Other herbs may pop up less frequently but we still wouldn't want to be without them. Cousin to oregano, marjoram is a wonderful garden plant with a far more pleasant flavor when used fresh. It is a natural with meats and accents seafood well, as you will see in the Marjoram Scented Mussels and Clams recipe.

Once a rarity, fennel pollen is going mainstream, leading to far lower prices than it used to fetch. I first came across it as a seasoning when I was taking a cooking class in Italy. That's when I learned how to make Renaissance Pork and, as part of the process, I fell in love with this pungent spice. One company calls it "fairy dust for chefs." You will find fennel pollen fun to play with, adding to roasted meats or sprinkling over veggies.

Dill seed, used here in the Cabbage and Chicken Sausage Supper, is another lesser-used but still important seasoning. The seed, more intense than the frilly dill weed, is a natural with cabbage and sauerkraut or green beans, carrots and, especially, pork.

Seasoning blends, those that you make yourself or buy already mixed, are handy at mealtime. Look for blends without salt or MSG so you get your money's worth in herbs and spices, not sodium; you can add salt if you so desire as you cook.

Curry powder, perhaps the most popular of the prepared blends, adds spice to vegetable dishes, soups, chicken and lamb. In the recipe for Curried Halibut in Paper, a complete meal is seasoned with curry. A zippy Cajun seasoning blend is used to season the Crawfish Fettuccini, but you could easily switch the two around making curried crawfish pasta or Cajun fish in paper.

Italian herb blends have many uses outside of spaghetti sauce. The typical combination of basil, oregano, thyme and garlic is perfect for beef stew, fish, or, as it is used here with other herbs and spices, in Mini Meatballs. These meatballs are terrific with traditional spaghetti and sauce, as well as filling meatball sandwiches. Meatballs are equally good in soups or sliced onto pizza.

Even more versatile is the Taco Meat Filling. You will find it as an ingredient in other chapters, used in the Taco Salad Buffet or as an optional topping on the Restaurant Nachos, but think of it for tostadas, baked potatoes and pizza, too.

Annatto seed, sometimes called achiote, is another of these earthy tastes. Annatto is what often gives butter and cheese their yellowish color, but we use it here to make an oil for coating a roasted Golden Chicken.

Black pepper is to savory foods what vanilla is to desserts. The spicy accent of peppercorns will rarely be the focus of a dish, but its absence is always noticed. Just a sprinkling at the end of cooking brightens a dish. Adding it early in the cooking process allows the black pepper bite to become a sultry undertone.

Not actually in the category of herbs or spices, intensely flavored condiments sometimes contribute as a seasoning. A splash of soy sauce or a bit of mustard can revive a bland dish. I like to use tamari instead of soy sauce because it seems less acrid. Along with sesame oil, tamari really makes the Seafood Spring Rolls pop, while mustard radiates robust flavor and a hint of heat in the Braised Pork Chops with Creamy Mustard Sauce.

These are recipes you can come back to again and again for family dinners or entertaining friends. They are dishes that are amenable to variations, allowing your own creativity to shine through.

Buffalo Stroganoff

Beef stroganoff has always been one of my favorite meals. I've "healthed" it up a bit here by using buffalo instead of beef and thick and tangy Greek yogurt to replace the traditional sour cream.

---

2 teaspoons vegetable oil
1 pound buffalo round steak, cut into ½x3-inch strips
1 medium yellow onion, chopped
2 cloves garlic, minced
1 cup beef broth
1 teaspoon dried thyme
¼ teaspoon freshly milled black pepper
Salt, to taste
2 Tablespoons flour
1 cup plain yogurt, preferably Greek-style
Hot cooked egg noodles or rice, for serving
2 Tablespoons minced parsley

Heat the oil in a large skillet over medium-high heat. Add half of the buffalo strips and brown on all sides; remove from pan. Brown the remaining strips. Return the first batch of browned buffalo to the pan and reduce the heat to medium; add the onion. Cook, stirring regularly, for about 3 minutes until the onion begins to soften. Stir in the garlic; cook another minute. Add the beef broth, thyme and pepper. Reduce heat to a simmer, cover and cook for 15 minutes, stirring occasionally. Uncover and continue simmering for 15 minutes more or until the liquid is reduced by half. Taste for salt and adjust seasonings, if desired.

Stir the flour into the yogurt. Remove the skillet from the heat and stir in the yogurt mixture. Return to low heat; heat through but do not boil. Serve over noodles or rice. Garnish with chopped parsley.

Makes 4 servings

Fajitas

This is a real crowd pleaser, and so delicious that you will be considered a culinary genius. When we invite friends for a fiesta, I like to make everything ahead of time except for grilling the meat so that I have plenty of time for visiting. If you would rather have chicken fajitas, follow the recipe but substitute lemon juice for lime juice in the marinade. For shrimp fajitas, use the chicken variation, but only marinate for 15 minutes.

½ cup Worcestershire sauce
Juice of one lime
½ teaspoon freshly milled black pepper
1 pound tri-tip steak
2 Tablespoons unsalted butter
2 large yellow onions, halved and sliced ½-inch wide
1 large bell pepper, halved, seeded and sliced into ½-inch strips
Salt and freshly milled black pepper
12 8-inch flour tortillas, warmed
1½ cups refried beans, warmed, optional
1 recipe Pico de Gallo, recipe follows
1 cup (4 ounces) shredded cheddar cheese
1 cup guacamole, or Poblano-Avocado Topping (page 19)
1 cup sour cream
1 cup salsa

Combine the Worcestershire sauce with the lime juice and black pepper in a sturdy ziplock plastic bag; add the meat. Marinate at least 4 hours or overnight in refrigerator.

Preheat the broiler or prepare a barbeque grill to cook the meat. Broil or grill as desired. After cooking, let the meat rest for about 10 minutes and slice into 1x3-inch strips; keep warm.

Meanwhile, melt the butter in a wide skillet. Add the onion and bell pepper strips; sauté until wilted and just beginning to brown, about 10 minutes. Season with salt and pepper.

To serve, arrange the cooked onion and bell pepper strips on a serving platter. Top with the cooked meat. Serve at the table with the flour tortillas and dishes of refried beans, if using, the pico de gallo, cheese, guacamole, sour cream and salsa. Allow guests to roll their own tacos.

Makes 6 servings

Pico de Gallo: Combine 1 seeded and stemmed minced jalapeno, 1 small minced yellow onion and 1 ripe finely chopped tomato. Add the juice of half a lime and season with a bit of salt to taste. Makes about 1½ cups salsa.

SAVORY ASIDE

Fresh from the prairie.

Buffalo is similar to beef yet lower in fat and calories plus higher in iron and protein. It is becoming widely available and quite popular. It's sometimes referred to as bison. You can find an assortment of cuts from steaks and roasts to ground meat or prepared sausages. Look for buffalo in the frozen meats department of your supermarket or ask your butcher to order it.

Taco Meat Filling

Toss out that envelope of prepared seasonings and artificial flavorings! This recipe, made from ingredients you probably have on hand, beats a mix any day. Ground buffalo is a terrific alternative to beef here. Consider taco meat for savory burritos, taco salads and the Restaurant Nachos on page 10.

---

1 pound ground beef
1 cup minced yellow onion
½ cup minced green bell pepper
1 clove garlic, minced
1 teaspoon ground cumin
½ teaspoon Mexican oregano
½ teaspoon salt
¼ teaspoon freshly milled black pepper
1 small tomato, cored and diced
½ cup water
2 Tablespoons cornmeal

Brown the hamburger in a medium skillet over medium-high heat, breaking up large clumps as it cooks; drain off fat. Return the cooked meat to the skillet; stir in the onion and bell pepper. Cook, stirring frequently, for 5 minutes. Add the garlic, cumin, oregano, salt and pepper. Reduce the heat to medium and cook, stirring occasionally, for 2 more minutes. Add the tomato and water; continue cooking, stirring occasionally, for another 10 minutes. Stir in the cornmeal to absorb liquids. Use meat filling in tacos or as desired.

Makes 3 cups

My Best Beef Jerky

Years ago we did a lot of camping and this beef jerky was always a welcome treat. It is much more toothsome than most commercial brands. The hardest part back then was regulating the oven to the proper temperature. These days ovens are more accurate so it's not as complicated.

2-3 pounds lean beef, like round steak
$^1/_3$ cup Worcestershire sauce
¼ cup tamari sauce
1½ teaspoons granulated onion
¾ teaspoon salt
½ teaspoon granulated garlic
½ teaspoon freshly milled black pepper
½ teaspoon hot Hungarian paprika
½ teaspoon dried lemon zest

Cut any visible fat or gristle from the beef. Slice across the grain into ½-inch wide strips about 6 inches long. Set aside.

Mix the remaining ingredients together in a deep glass bowl or sturdy ziplock plastic bag. Add the meat strips; toss well to coat. Cover bowl with plastic wrap or seal bag tight and refrigerate 24 to 48 hours. Toss the mixture every now and then while marinating.

Using an oven thermometer, heat the oven to 170 degrees (F).

Transfer the meat strips to a rack and pan that will allow air to circulate and catch drips from the marinade. The strips may touch each other but should not overlap.

Place the rack/pan in the center of the oven and allow to dry for about 10 hours. Start watching after 8 or 9 hours since drying times will vary. When finished, the strips will be pliable but dry in appearance. Store in an airtight container.

Makes 12 ounces

Calzones

The ingredient list is long and so are the instructions, but once you get the hang of making calzones you will see how easy and versatile they are. This sausage, onion and bell pepper filling is classic, however anything your little heart desires will work. In fact, you can make everyone happy by using a different filling for each diner, if you want. Just be sure to use the cheeses and to replace the sausage and onion with equal amounts of other meats and veggies. Keep track of which one is which by cutting different marks on top when you make the vents. These freeze beautifully. After baking and cooling, wrap well and freeze. Reheat, without thawing, by covering the calzones with foil on a baking sheet in a preheated 375-degree oven for about 35 minutes.

For the dough:
1 cup warm water (110-115 degrees)
2¼ teaspoons active dry yeast
2¼ cups semolina
1 cup all-purpose flour
¼ cup olive oil
½ teaspoon salt
Cornmeal for preparing pan

For the filling:
12 ounces Italian sausage, casings removed if necessary
2 teaspoons olive oil
1 small yellow onion, sliced
½ of a green bell pepper, sliced
½ of a red bell pepper, sliced
1 teaspoon Italian herb blend
3 cups (12 ounces) mozzarella cheese, shredded
1 cup (8 ounces) ricotta cheese
½ cup (2 ounces) Parmesan cheese, shredded

For serving:
3 cups hot pasta sauce

To prepare the dough: In a food processor fitted with the steel blade, whirl the water with the yeast just to blend; allow to sit for 5 minutes, or until small bubbles indicate the yeast is active. Add the remaining dough ingredients, in the order given, to the yeasted water. Process with pulses until well combined and the dough forms a ball. (Sometimes this won't happen, but it will still be ready. The key is when you pinch the dough, it will hold together. You may need to add a bit more flour or a bit more water.) Remove the dough from the food processor bowl (a light coat of non-stick spray on your hands makes this easier) and knead it briefly then form into a smooth ball. Place in an oiled bowl, turning to coat with the oil. Cover the bowl with plastic wrap. Set aside to rise in a warm, draft-free place for about 45 minutes, or until it has doubled in bulk.

To prepare the filling: While the dough rises, prepare the filling. Cook the sausage over medium-high heat, breaking it up into small pieces, until it is cooked through and beginning to brown. Drain on paper toweling and set aside.

Return the pan to the heat with the 2 teaspoons of oil. Add the onions and bell peppers; sauté until the onion is translucent. Sprinkle with the Italian herbs and cook another couple of minutes. Set aside to cool.

Preheat the oven to 425 degrees.

To assemble the calzones: Divide the dough into six equal pieces. Roll each piece into a 10-inch circle. Sprinkle a large baking sheet, preferably one without sides, with a light coating of cornmeal. Arrange each circle on the baking sheet so that half of it lies over the side.

Leaving a half-inch edge, use half of the shredded mozzarella to make a layer of cheese on each half-moon of dough on the baking sheet. Top each layer of cheese with equal portions of the sausage and the onion and bell peppers. Use a teaspoon to distribute equal amounts of the ricotta over the sausage and onions on each calzone. Sprinkle each with 1½ Tablespoons of the Parmesan and top with the remaining mozzarella in an even layer.

Now fold the unfilled dough over the top of the filling to make half circles, tucking in the filling as necessary. Using your thumb and forefingers, pinch the dough and push your thumbs together to get a good seal. Once sealed, use a sharp knife to cut two or three vents into the top of the dough.

Bake for 20 to 25 minutes, until the tops are nicely browned. Serve each calzone with ½ cup of the pasta sauce on the side.

Makes 6 calzones

Mini Meatballs

Meatballs make me happy. I like them with pasta, of course, but they are also an ingredient in my all-time favorite pizza: sliced meatballs, red onions and jalapenos with smoked mozzarella. You can make them any size you want, just bake them a bit longer if you go larger. Since we can't taste the recipe for seasoning because of the raw meat, you might want to fry a bit of the mixture up to sample before cooking them all. Meatballs freeze well, too. Freeze them in a single layer, then gather them up and store in a plastic freezer bag.

---

1 cup soft breadcrumbs
½ cup milk
¾ pound ground beef
¼ pound ground pork
¼ pound ground veal
1 large egg
4 teaspoons Italian herbs blend
1 Tablespoon dried parsley
1 Tablespoon dried minced onion (if making large meatballs, use 2 Tablespoons freshly minced onion)
1 teaspoon whole fennel seed
½ teaspoon dry mustard
½ teaspoon salt
¼ teaspoon freshly milled black pepper

Soak the breadcrumbs in the milk for 10 minutes. Preheat the oven to 350 degrees. Oil a large baking sheet with sides, or coat it with non-stick spray.

Squeeze excess milk from the soaking breadcrumbs and place the crumbs in a large bowl along with the remaining ingredients. Mix thoroughly with your hands. Roll this meat mixture into small balls, using about 2 teaspoons to create balls roughly the diameter of a quarter. Place at intervals, close but not touching, on the baking sheet.

Bake for 12 minutes. Before removing from oven, test for doneness by cutting one in half. If it's no longer pink in the center, they are finished cooking. If it is still pink, cook for a couple of minutes longer, keeping a close watch so they don't burn.

Makes 70 one-inch meatballs

Renaissance Pork

I first tasted this delectable dish at Casa Caponetti Cooking School in Tuscania, Italy. Although Mrs. Caponetti seasoned a succulent local pork roast with the delicate grains of wild fennel pollen to perfection, I have had excellent results in preparing it with plain old fennel seed in my American kitchen. She suggested that our pork in the States doesn't have as much flavor as the Italian meat because we trim off so much fat. This is one time I break my general rule of going lean.

---

3 firm pears, cored and sliced ½-inch thick
2 yellow onions, peeled, halved and sliced ¼-inch thick
2 Tablespoons olive oil, plus more for roasting pan
1 pork roast, about 3 pounds, with plenty of fat
6 cloves garlic, unpeeled
3 teaspoons crushed fennel seed (or use fennel pollen)
1 teaspoon kosher salt
1 teaspoon cracked black pepper

Preheat the oven to 325 degrees.

Oil a roasting pan and add the pears and onions. Drizzle with the olive oil; toss to coat.

Cut six slits into the roast at even intervals. Insert a garlic clove into each slit. Mix together the fennel, salt and pepper; rub evenly onto the roast. Place on an oiled rack in the roasting pan over the pears and onions.

Roast the pork for about 1½ to 2 hours or until a meat thermometer reads 150 degrees. Allow the roast to rest on a warmed plate tented with foil for 15 minutes before slicing.

Makes about 6 servings

Braised Pork Chops with Creamy Mustard Sauce

This is such a homey dish, perfect with noodles on the side along with green beans or limas. Upon sampling this, one of the recipe testers said, "I am so buying this book."

---

1 Tablespoon olive oil
6 (3 ounces each) pork loin chops
3 teaspoons fresh minced thyme, divided
Salt and freshly milled pepper, to taste
1 medium yellow onion, quartered and thinly sliced
⅓ cup orange juice
¼ cup water
¼ cup sour cream
2 Tablespoons Dijon-style mustard
Sprigs of fresh thyme, for garnish

Heat the oil in a large skillet over medium-high heat. Add the pork chops and season with 1 teaspoon of the thyme and salt and pepper. Brown well on one side before turning over to begin browning the other side. After turning, scatter the onion in the skillet around the pork, stirring a bit to coat with oil. When the pork chops are thoroughly browned, reduce heat to medium-low.

Add the orange juice, water and remaining 2 teaspoons of thyme to the skillet. Bring to a simmer and cover. Continue cooking at a slow simmer for 15 minutes. Uncover and continue simmering until about half of the liquid has evaporated, five minutes or so. Meanwhile, combine the sour cream and mustard in a small bowl.

Transfer the pork chops to a warmed plate. Remove the skillet from the heat and gently stir in the sour cream/mustard mixture. Reduce the heat to very low and return the skillet to stove. Return pork chops to skillet and cover; heat the sauce but be sure it does not boil.

To serve, place pork chops on a serving platter and pour the sauce over top. Garnish the plate with the thyme sprigs.

Makes 4 servings

Pesto Pork Chops

A schmear of pesto takes a simple, broiled chop to new levels. As the pork chops finish cooking, the pesto bubbles into an attractive and absolutely delicious accent.

---

4 boneless pork loin chops, 1-inch thick
Kosher salt and freshly milled black pepper
¼ cup prepared pesto (pages 212-214)

Preheat broiler unit. Coat a broiling pan and rack with non-stick cooking spray.

Trim any excess fat from the pork chops and season both sides with salt and pepper; place on broiling rack.

Broil the chops about 5 inches away from the heat source until the tops are nicely browned, about 8 minutes. Turn them over and continue cooking 5 minutes more or until cooked through.

Remove from heat and spread each chop evenly with 1 Tablespoon of pesto. Return to the broiler and cook until the pesto just begins to bubble and brown, about 3 minutes. Allow to rest, tented with foil, for 5 minutes before serving.

Makes 4 servings

Cabbage and Chicken Sausage Supper

I love to serve steamed new potatoes alongside salmon or other fish but often have leftovers. This quick skillet dinner is a great way to use them up. If you must start from scratch, steam the potatoes for about 30 minutes or until fork tender. Allow to cool completely before proceeding with the recipe. The green beans are a little large if you use them right from the can, so I always run a sharp knife through the can a couple of times after draining.

---

1 Tablespoon olive oil
1 medium yellow onion, chopped
1 teaspoon dill seeds
2 links (about 3 ounces each) fully-cooked chicken-apple sausage, (or something similar) halved lengthwise and cut into ¼-inch thick slices
½ head of cabbage, chopped (about 4 cups)
1 can (15 ounces) green beans, drained
²/₃ pound cold steamed potatoes, peeled if desired and cut into ½-inch cubes
½ teaspoon salt
½ teaspoon freshly milled black pepper
¼ cup chopped parsley

Heat the oil over medium-high heat in a wide skillet. Add the onions and cook, stirring regularly, for 3-5 minutes until softened. Stir in the dill seeds and cook another minute more. Add the sausage, cabbage, green beans, potatoes, salt and pepper. Stir well. Reduce heat to medium-low; cover and cook, stirring occasionally, for 10 minutes, or until the cabbage is wilted and the sausage is heated through.

To serve, arrange on a large platter and sprinkle with the chopped parsley.

Makes 2 large servings

SAVORY ASIDE

Terms of purchase.

When perusing spice catalogs you may come across unfamiliar terms for how each item is offered. Whole or ground is the most common and also the most logical. An example of a whole spice is a single nutmeg or cardamom still in the pod. When they are ground, we get a powdered form although some are coarser than others. The term "cut and sifted" usually refers to herbs that have been chopped and run through a sieve to remove stems. If a form is not specified, an herb is likely in whole leaf form like thyme or rosemary. Granulated equates to the consistency of sugar.

A Golden Chicken

There is something cozy about a whole roasted chicken. This one is downright pretty, too, with its crisp skin a deep golden color from the annatto oil. Keep the Latin theme by serving it with Corn and Black Bean Salad with Tortilla Strip Croutons (page 166). Or go traditional and serve the chicken with mashed potatoes and Skillet Steamed Swiss Chard (page 147).

---

1 teaspoon Mexican oregano
½ teaspoon kosher salt
¼ teaspoon freshly milled black pepper
1 4-5 pound roasting chicken
2 small bay leaves
¼ cup annatto oil (page 211)

Preheat the oven to 375 degrees.

In a small bowl, combine the oregano, salt and pepper.

Rinse the chicken and pat dry. Sprinkle the spice mixture into the breast cavity and add the bay leaves. Place the bird on a rack in a roasting pan. Brush skin well with annatto oil.

Roast the chicken for 45-50 minutes or until juices run clear when pricked.

Makes 4 servings with tasty leftovers

Herbed Chicken Pot Pie

Few things in life make my husband happier than tucking into a steaming chicken pot pie. I often make a whole roasted chicken one night and then use up the leftovers in this recipe a few nights later. It's also wonderful with the turkey that you have in the freezer from Thanksgiving dinner. If your chicken (or turkey) is already cooked, skip the first step that involves poaching the meat and pick up by making a little herb broth for cooking the potatoes and carrots. Please don't be intimidated by the long recipe. It is really just three steps: cooking the chicken and veggies, making the sauce, and preparing the topping. Your effort will be well worth the reward.

½ pound boneless chicken breast
3 four-inch sprigs of fresh thyme, plus 2½ teaspoons chopped fresh
2 four-inch sprigs of fresh rosemary, divided
4 whole peppercorns
2 medium red or gold potatoes, peeled and cubed small
1 medium carrot, diced
1 teaspoon salt, divided
$^1/_3$ cup peas, thawed if frozen
1 cup milk
2 Tablespoons unsalted butter
¼ of a large yellow onion, minced
1 stalk of celery, minced
2 Tablespoons, plus 1 cup all-purpose flour
2 dashes cayenne pepper
2 Tablespoons minced fresh parsley, divided
1 teaspoon baking powder
½ teaspoon salt
½ teaspoon baking soda
¼ cup shortening (look for a zero trans-fat variety)
½ cup buttermilk

Poach the chicken by placing it in a saucepan with the 3 sprigs of thyme, 1 sprig of rosemary, the peppercorns and just enough water to barely cover the chicken. Bring to a simmer; reduce heat slightly and cover. Poach for about 7 minutes, turn the chicken over and continue simmering another 7 minutes, or until the chicken is cooked through. Remove the chicken breast and set it aside. Save the cooking liquid for the next step. Remove the whole peppercorns and discard.

Add the potatoes and carrots to the poaching water with the other sprig of rosemary and ½ teaspoon of the salt. If necessary, add more water to cover the vegetables; bring to a boil. Cook until the potatoes are nearly tender, about 10 minutes; add the peas and continue cooking until the potatoes are soft. Strain 1 cup of the potato/carrot cooking liquid into a 2-cup measuring cup, discard remaining liquid. Add the milk to fill the cup to the 2-cup mark. Remove the herbs stems from the potatoes and carrots. When the chicken is cool enough to handle, shred it into small pieces with two forks or your fingers.

Melt the butter in a saucepan over medium heat. Stir in the onion, celery and ½ teaspoon of the chopped thyme. Cook, stirring occasionally, until the vegetables are tender, about 5 minutes. Sprinkle in the 2 Tablespoons of flour; mix well. Cook and stir for about 3 minutes. Slowly stir in the reserved water and milk mixture with 1 teaspoon of the chopped thyme, the cayenne and 1 Tablespoon of the parsley. Continue to cook until the mixture thickens. Season with salt and pepper to taste. Stir in the reserved potato/carrot mixture and the chicken, adding a bit more milk if the mixture seems too thick. Pour the pot pie filling into a buttered 2-quart baking dish. Cover with foil to keep warm while you make the topping.

Preheat the oven to 425 degrees.

To make the biscuit topping, combine the 1 cup flour with the remaining 1 teaspoon of chopped thyme and 1 Tablespoon parsley, the baking powder, salt and baking soda. Cut in the shortening with a fork until the mixture resembles coarse crumbs. Quickly stir in the buttermilk until the mixture is just moistened. Turn out onto a piece of floured waxed paper; knead briefly. Form the dough into a 6-inch square that is ¼-inch thick and then cut into 12 square biscuits with a floured knife. Arrange these biscuit squares on top of the pot pie filling leaving, a bit of space between each one.

Bake the pot pie for about 12 minutes, or until the mixture is bubbly and the biscuit topping is beginning to brown. Serve right away.

Makes 4 servings

Turkey-Arugula Melt

Nothing beats arugula you grow yourself, but you can often find it at the farmers' market during the summer or year round in the supermarket. This tasty open-faced sandwich is delicious with the chipotle mayonnaise, although you could use Thousand Island Dressing (page 209) or your favorite sandwich spread if you can't take the heat. Fontina is my favorite melting cheese but your favorite will certainly work, too.

---

1 thick slice whole grain or rye bread
1 Tablespoon chipotle mayonnaise, recipe follows
½ cup packed arugula leaves
3 ounces thinly sliced smoked turkey
1 slice Fontina cheese

Preheat the broiler. On a baking sheet, layer the ingredients in the order given. Place under the broiler about 5 inches away from the heat source and allow the cheese to melt and become bubbly. Serve right away with a knife and fork.

Makes 1 sandwich

Chipotle Mayonnaise: Combine ½ cup mayonnaise with 1 teaspoon minced chipotle chile in adobo sauce, or use chipotle paste. This will keep for weeks in the refrigerator.

Curried Halibut in Paper

Parchment paper used in this recipe can be found in most supermarkets. In a pinch, foil may be used with less dramatic results. This preparation works with most any fish; halibut is my favorite.

---

2 teaspoons olive oil
1 cup packed spinach leaves, washed, stemmed and torn, if large
2 (6 ounces each) skinless halibut fillets
Salt and freshly milled black pepper, to taste
2 teaspoons curry powder
1 small tomato, cored and sliced thin

Preheat the oven to 400 degrees.

Cut two sheets of parchment paper measuring approximately 16x12-inches each. Fold each sheet in half and cut out a large half heart to form a heart-shaped piece of parchment when you open it.

Brush the center of each half of the heart shapes lightly with olive oil. Divide the spinach leaves between the two pieces of parchment, arranging in a layer on the oiled center. Season the fish with salt and pepper then rub 1 teaspoon of curry powder over both sides of each fillet. Place the fish on top of the spinach bed. Arrange the tomato slices so that they overlap atop the fish fillets. To seal the package, fold the other half of the parchment paper heart over the fish. Beginning at the rounded end, fold over about an inch of the edge and press down hard. Take the next inch, overlapping slightly and fold it over, moving around to the pointed end, creating a tight seal.

Place the baking sheet in the oven and bake 10 minutes for each inch thickness of the fish. To serve, place the unopened parchment packet onto the serving plate, snip a hole in the center and allow each diner to tear into his or her own entrée, but watch out for steam.

Makes 2 servings

Tropical Fish

I like to make this with snapper because I can usually find it fresh and the fillets are small so they cook quickly before the coconut burns. You could use other firm-fleshed white fish. Whatever you choose, don't forget to check for pin bones. I always use a pair of tweezers to remove the little bones but often make a mess of it. Good thing the coconut breading covers that up.

1 cup shredded, unsweetened coconut
1 cup panko bread crumbs
¾ cup all-purpose flour
2 eggs
¼ cup olive oil, divided
8 (3 ounces each) skinless snapper fillets
Salt and freshly milled black pepper, to taste
Tropical Salsa, for garnish, recipe follows

Toast the coconut by shaking it in a dry skillet over medium-high heat until it is slightly browned. Allow to cool on a plate before using.

Combine the coconut and panko on a sheet of wax paper. Place the flour on a second sheet of wax paper. Crack the eggs into a shallow bowl and stir well to break them up. Heat 2 Tablespoons of oil in a wide skillet over medium-high heat. Set the oven to warm.

Season the snapper fillets with salt and pepper. To bread the fish, dip each one first into the flour to coat lightly and then dip it into the beaten egg; allow excess to drip off then transfer the fillet to the coconut-panko mixture. Press the crumbs onto the fillet, shaking lightly to remove the excess.

When the oil is shimmering, add as many fillets as the skillet will hold. Cook for about 3 minutes, or until the breading is golden brown. Turn, cook 3 minutes more, or until the breading is golden brown and the fish is cooked through. Transfer to a plate; hold in the oven while you cook the remaining fillets, adding more oil to the pan skillet as necessary.

To serve, arrange two fillets on each of four serving plates and top with the Tropical Salsa.

Makes 4 servings

Curry-Garbanzo variation: Combine 1/2 cup garbanzo bean flour and 2 teaspoons curry powder on a sheet of wax paper and use this to coat the fillets instead of the coconut-panko breading.

Tropical Salsa

This sunny garnish takes your fish, or chicken, on a trip to the islands. Regular coarse salt will work if you don't have any of the Hawaiian variety on hand. Try this salsa on fish tacos, too.

---

1 cup diced ripe, but firm, banana
½ cup minced fresh pineapple
½ cup minced red onion
1 jalapeno, stemmed, seeded and minced
Juice from 1 lime
½ teaspoon Hawaiian red sea salt

Combine the banana, pineapple, red onion and jalapeno in a medium bowl. Add the lime juice and salt; toss well.

Makes 2 cups

Seafood Spring Rolls

Here's a quick, low-fat lunch or snack that helps to sneak a few more veggies into the day. It's also a great way to use up the little snippets of different things that end up in the refrigerator vegetable bin. You might consider adding snow peas, water chestnuts or bean sprouts. If you need to use regular head cabbage it will take a bit longer to cook.

---

1 Tablespoon peanut oil
1-inch piece of ginger, peeled and minced
1 clove garlic, minced
1 small head of Savoy or Napa cabbage, cored and sliced into thin strips (about 2½ cups)
1 small carrot, grated
½ cup red or green bell pepper strips (¼-inch wide)
3 green onions, sliced, white and green parts separated
1 cup tiny shrimp or chopped langoustines or crab meat
5 teaspoons tamari, divided
1 teaspoon toasted sesame oil
12-15 spring roll wraps (aka skins)
Your favorite Asian sauce for dipping

Heat the oil in a wide skillet or wok over medium-high heat. Once it is shimmering, add the ginger and garlic; cook and stir for about 30 seconds, or until fragrant. Stir in the cabbage, carrot, bell pepper and white parts of the green onion. Continue to cook, stirring almost constantly, until the vegetables are softened, about 5 minutes. Add the shrimp and 3 teaspoons of the tamari. The shrimp (or other seafood) may release a bit of water. Cook, stirring often, until the excess liquid has evaporated. Remove from the heat, toss in the green parts of the green onions and season with the remaining 2 teaspoons of tamari and the sesame oil. Taste and adjust seasonings as necessary. *(Can be made ahead to this point. Keep covered in the refrigerator for no more than a day or two; bring to room temperature before proceeding.)*

To make the rolls, soften a single skin at a time in a dish of hot water until it is pliable, about 45 seconds. Transfer the softened skin to a dry, folded dish towel on your work surface, turn once to dry both sides. Spoon 1 heaping Tablespoon of the cabbage filling in a strip down the center of the skin, leaving about half an inch border near the edges. Fold those edges in, to make more of a rectangle. Fold one rounded side over the other, pulling the filling in tightly and then roll into a thin cylinder. (This is awkward the first couple of tries but you'll get the hang of it.) Place on a serving platter and continue to roll the remaining skins and fillings. Don't allow the rolls to touch on the serving plate or they may stick together.

Serve right away with a small dish of sauce for dipping.

Makes 12 to 15 rolls

Crawfish Fettuccini

Crawfish could quite possibly be the best part of living in Southern Louisiana. These succulent little shellfish are only available fresh at certain times of the year. I always had to buy them cooked because to get them live you had to purchase 30 pounds minimum. If you don't have access to freshly caught crawfish, you might find them frozen as 'peeled crawfish tails' or substitute shrimp or rock lobster.

---

1 Tablespoon olive oil
1 Tablespoon unsalted butter
1 small yellow onion, minced
½ of a green bell pepper, minced
1 stalk celery, minced
1 clove garlic, minced
1½ teaspoons no-salt-added Cajun spices, divided
2 Tablespoons all-purpose flour
2 cups hot milk
1 pound peeled crawfish tails
1 pound cooked warm fettuccini
2 green onions, sliced
Tabasco sauce, optional

Heat the olive oil and butter together in a medium skillet over medium-high heat. Stir in the onion, bell pepper and celery. Cook, stirring regularly, for 3-4 minutes. Add the garlic and ½ teaspoon of the Cajun spices and cook 2-3 minutes longer. Stir in the flour; continue to cook and stir 3 more minutes. Gradually add the milk, breaking up any lumps that may form. Bring to a boil; reduce the heat to maintain a simmer. Stir in the remaining teaspoon of Cajun spices and the crawfish. Simmer, stirring regularly, until the sauce thickens and the crawfish is heated through.

Pour over the fettuccini, sprinkle with the green onions and serve immediately. Pass the Tabasco sauce, if desired, for those who like it hotter.

Makes about 4 servings

Sashimi-Shiso Wraps

This is inspired by a wondrous meal we happened upon by accident in Seoul, South Korea. Of the 32 dishes that landed on our table during a meal that involved fish tanks on the sidewalk, these shiso wraps were our favorite. If I couldn't identify a species of fish or shellfish (and I use that term loosely), our host would march me outside and point to the holding tank filled with that particular delicacy. His wife showed us how to fill and roll the shiso leaves. You might need to grow shiso, a Japanese herb, if you want to enjoy its somewhat spicy cinnamon basil flavor. In the town of Inchon, they grow large quantities of shiso on vacant lots in neighborhoods.

16 large fresh whole shiso leaves, stems removed
4 ounces sushi-grade raw fish, cut into 16 thin slices
Pickled ginger
Sriracha Chili Sauce

Using a shiso leaf as the base, add one piece of fish, a slice of pickled ginger and a dab of the Sriracha (use caution—it's hot!). Roll the leaf to enclose the fillings. Place on a serving dish, seam side down, or eat them as you roll them.

Makes 16

Marjoram Scented Mussels and Clams

This is summer cooking at its finest and a great way to use up that little bit of leftover white wine. It may not seem like enough liquid to start with, but as you will see, the mussels and clams release a good bit of their own "liquor" as they cook. You couldn't go wrong by serving a side of Turmeric Pasta (page 220) with it for soaking up all that goodness. We prepared this recipe in a crab pot on a gas grill during a boat outing and it worked like a charm.

1½ pounds of mussels, scrubbed and debearded
2 pounds Manila clams
1 lemon, sliced thick
4 8-inch sprigs of marjoram
2 6-inch sprigs of tarragon, optional
¾ cup dry white wine

Put the mussels and clams into a deep pot with a tight fitting lid. Drop in the lemon slices, ends and all, plus the marjoram and tarragon, if using. Pour the wine over all. Set the pot over high heat and bring to a boil. Reduce the heat slightly and steam until all of the shellfish have opened, about 10 minutes.

Discard the lemon and herbs; transfer the shellfish and steaming liquid to a large bowl and serve right away.

Makes 4 servings

Rice and Lentil Combo Plate, page 127

Main Dish Meals: For the flexitarian in all of us

The word flexitarian entered our lexicon in 1992 as a way to describe a vegetarian who occasionally eats meat or fish. I find that including meatless main dishes in the mix each week is a pleasant way to get more veggies and grains into my diet. Herbs and spices make these dishes even more interesting and varied.

Curry powder is a great example. We use the highly spiced blend twice in this chapter. In Curried Vegetables, an otherwise pedestrian plate of fresh veggies is transformed into a tantalizing, creamy concoction. Even if you use the same curry powder, the flavor of the Curried Millet Bowl with Spinach and Garbanzos is a completely different meal. A hint of sweetness from the chutney plays off of the robust curry so well.

Hundreds of curry powders are available commercially in varying degrees of heat. Or you might make your own. Common spices in curry are cumin and coriander, ginger and cardamom, different peppers, black and red, maybe mustard and cinnamon. Turmeric is the spice that gives the characteristic yellow color.

You will find cooking with spices even more rewarding if you buy them whole and grind them yourself. A coffee grinder dedicated to this purpose makes quick work of reducing them to a powder and gives a more consistent texture than using a mortar and pestle. Whole spices last longer than those that are purchased already ground, too, so you get more bang for your buck.

Sometimes you don't have a choice of whole or ground spices. This is usually the case with sumac, a Middle Eastern spice often referred to as a souring agent. The berries of the sumac plant are almost always sold in a coarsely ground stage. We use the reddish, brown powder in the Rice and Lentil Combo Plate for a pleasant tart highlight. Look for sumac in the classic za'atar blend on page 16, as well.

From the Middle East to points around the globe, vegetarian recipes allow you to explore the world. Fried Rice, savory from the addition of sesame oil and tamari, gives us a taste of the Orient while Kasha in Acorn Squash Bowls takes us to Eastern Europe. Crispy Chile Rellenos or the cumin-laced Double Bean and Spinach Stew illustrate the heartiness of the great Southwestern United States.

Put your basil leaves to work in the Italian-inspired Eggplant Extra. Basil is such a wonderful herb when used fresh that it actually merits growing more than one plant. Like most plants, basil thrives on being snipped back. By pinching or cutting the soft stems at a place just above where a leaf pair emerges, the plant is encouraged to grow and become bushy rather than tall. In addition to making pestos and Italian dishes, think of tucking the leaves into sandwiches, using them as one of the greens in a tossed salad or as part of an omelet filling.

Regardless of whether you consider yourself a flexitarian or not, you will find these recipes tasty and satisfying. And the best part is that you'll never miss the meat.

Curried Vegetables

I like to make this quick and tasty dish for lunch when I've got some brown rice already cooked. Any combination of vegetables will work, so feel free to use what you've got on hand. This curry reheats very well, although you may need to add a bit more cream if it's too thick.

---

1 Tablespoon olive oil
1 small onion, chopped
1 Tablespoon curry powder
1 medium carrot, sliced
½ red bell pepper, chopped
¼ head cauliflower, sliced
1 small zucchini, cut into half moons
½ cup peas
Salt to taste
¾ cup heavy cream
Hot cooked rice, for serving
1 small tomato, chopped

Heat the oil in a wok pan or skillet until shimmering. Add the onion, cook and stir 2 minutes. Sprinkle the curry powder over the onions; cook and stir for 30 seconds. Add the carrot, bell pepper and cauliflower. Cook for 5 minutes, stirring almost constantly. Stir in the zucchini and peas; season the vegetables with salt. Pour in the cream; bring to a boil. Continue cooking until the cream has reduced and thickened slightly and the vegetables are soft.

To serve, ladle over rice and sprinkle with the chopped tomatoes.

Makes 2 to 4 servings

Crispy Chile Rellenos

This is my copycat recipe of a dish prepared at the popular Moosehill Cantina in Lakewood, Colorado. Traditional rellenos are enveloped in a fluffy egg batter, but these little gems are wrapped up like an egg roll and cooked crispy. Don't sauce them until just before eating to maintain that crispiness. Spanish Rice (page 160), refried beans and a small avocado side salad make these a great meal.

---

6 ounces Pepper-Jack cheese, at room temperature
12 Anaheim chiles, roasted (page 221)
12 egg roll wrappers
Vegetable oil for frying
2 cups Enchilada Sauce (page 208)

Slice the cheese into 12 rectangles that are ½-inch thick and measure 1x2½-inches.

To assemble the rellenos, lay one chile out flat. Place one piece of cheese in center. Fold the chile around to enclose the cheese. Lay one egg roll wrapper out in a diamond shape. Brush a little water over the edges to serve as "glue" for the finished relleno. Place the chile-wrapped cheese into center of wrapper and fold up envelope-style, beginning by pulling up the bottom point over the chile. Fold in the sides and then bring the top point down to make a neat rectangle. Repeat with remaining ingredients to form 11 more chile rellenos.

Heat 1 inch of oil in a heavy skillet until very hot but not smoking. Carefully place 3 chile rellenos into the oil and cook for about 2 minutes or until crispy. Turn them over; fry 2 minutes more until both sides are crispy. Remove from oil with a slotted spoon; drain on paper towels. Repeat with remaining rellenos.

To serve, place 3 chile rellenos on a plate and top with ½ cup warmed Enchilada Sauce.

Makes 4 servings

Fennel Ravioli with a Simple Tomato Sauce

This is a recipe that my friend and I developed after we made our own ricotta cheese. I know fennel pollen is an unusual ingredient but I think you will find many uses for it if you make the small investment. It's delicious sprinkled over vegetables or pork and chicken. You can substitute ground fennel seed.

For the filling:
1 container (15 ounces) ricotta cheese
¼ cup freshly grated Parmesan cheese
2 heaping Tablespoons minced fresh dill
1 large egg
½ teaspoon salt
$^1/_8$ teaspoon freshly milled black pepper

For the pasta:
1 cup semolina
1 cup all-purpose flour
¾ teaspoon fennel pollen (or ground fennel seed)
$^1/_8$ teaspoon salt
½ cup warm water, plus more as needed
1 large egg, beaten

For the sauce:
3 Tablespoons olive oil
2 large shallots, thinly sliced
2 cans (15 ounces) diced tomatoes in juice, "petite cut" if available
1 Tablespoon minced fresh parsley
Extra virgin olive oil, for garnish, if desired
Chopped parsley, for garnish, if desired

Combine the filling ingredients in a small bowl; set aside.

To make the pasta, toss the dry ingredients together in a medium mixing bowl. Stir in the ½ cup water. When the mixture is too stiff to stir with a spoon, begin kneading in more water, 1 Tablespoon at a time, to form a firm but pliable dough.

If rolling the dough out by hand, continue kneading a few minutes more. Wrap in plastic and allow to rest for 30 minutes. Divide into four or more portions and roll to desired thickness (see below) with a rolling pin. Keep extra dough covered.

If rolling the dough through a machine or hand-cranked roller, wrap in plastic and allow to rest for 30 minutes. Divide dough into four or more portions; keep them covered when you are not working them. Knead the dough by feeding each portion into the machine set on the largest number several times, folding the dough into thirds after each time through. Roll the dough by reducing the thickness in small increments.

Roll each portion into a paper-thin strip 4½-inches wide. Brush lightly with the beaten egg. Place heaping teaspoonfuls of the filling along the bottom half of the strip leaving 1-inch between each teaspoon of filling. Fold the top half of the dough down over the filling. Use the sides of your hands to cup the filling and expel as much air as possible before pressing down edges to seal. Use a pastry wheel, or pizza cutter, to even up the edges, then roll the cutter between each ravioli. Check to make sure they are well sealed as you transfer them to a baking sheet lined with parchment paper. Continue until you have used all of the filling. Bring a large pot of salted water to a boil as you prepare the sauce.

In a large skillet over medium heat, heat the olive oil until it shimmers. Stir in the shallots. Cook, stirring almost constantly, until the shallots begin to brown. Stir in the canned tomatoes and parsley. Reduce the heat and keep warm until the ravioli is ready.

Adjust the heat under the boiling water to maintain a strong simmer. Carefully drop in the ravioli, 8 to 12 at a time. Cook for 3 minutes, stirring gently every now and then. Remove the cooked ravioli with a slotted spoon and serve right away as follows. (Uncooked ravioli can be held in the refrigerator for a couple of days or frozen.)

To serve, spoon a bit of the tomato sauce into a pasta bowl. Top with 6 to 8 ravioli and spoon a bit more sauce over them. Drizzle with the extra virgin olive oil and parsley, if using.

Makes 4 servings (4 dozen ravioli)

Pesto Pasta II

This zesty, colorful concoction will make you popular at the next potluck. I recommend using the Cooking School Pesto (page 214) for this recipe. Since it doesn't have as much garlic, the taste of the pesto complements rather than competes with the other strong flavors. This is best served right away or at room temperature.

---

2 Tablespoons pesto
4 ounces (about 2 cups) dried pasta spirals
1$^{1}/_{3}$ cups (two 6½-ounce jars) chopped artichoke hearts
$^{2}/_{3}$ cup (about 25 whole) sliced black olives
2 small Roma tomatoes, cored and chopped
¼ cup freshly grated Parmesan cheese
$^{1}/_{8}$ teaspoon freshly milled black pepper

Place the pesto in a large mixing bowl.

Cook the pasta according to the package directions. Before draining, measure out 1 Tablespoon of the cooking water and add to the pesto.

Stir the drained hot pasta with the pesto and mix until the noodles are coated. Add the artichokes, olives and tomatoes; toss gently but thoroughly.

Transfer to a serving dish. Sprinkle with cheese, then the black pepper.

Makes 6 cups

Double Bean Spinach Stew

This hearty stew is a meal on its own, but I really enjoy it with some kind of corn. Polenta is great or consider Corn Cakes (page 18) or an ear of corn. If there was ever a recipe that allows for dabbling, this is it. Add a bit of sausage or bacon if you are feeling carnivorous. Use kidney beans and white beans instead of the blacks and reds. Even the spinach is dispensable if you want to substitute kale, chard or mustard greens. Frozen greens will work, too. Whatever you choose, be sure to chop up the leaves. I have tried just tossing them in whole with poor results; you end up with globs of greens that don't cook evenly or mesh with the other ingredients. The pickled jalapenos really do make the dish, however, so add more or don't use as many, but do put them in.

---

1 Tablespoon vegetable oil
1 large yellow onion, chopped
1 fat clove garlic, minced
2 Tablespoons ground cumin
2 heaping Tablespoons chopped pickled jalapenos
1 can (15 ounces) black beans, undrained
1 can (15 ounces) small red beans, undrained
1 bunch spinach, washed well and roughly chopped
½ teaspoon salt or more, to taste

Heat the oil in a large skillet over medium-high heat. Add the onion; cook, stirring often, until translucent and just beginning to brown, about 8 minutes. Stir in the garlic, cumin and jalapenos. Cook and stir for a minute or so. Stir in the beans with their liquid. Reduce the heat to medium and add the spinach and salt. Cover the skillet and allow the spinach to steam. Stir every couple of minutes, cooking until the spinach is well wilted into the stew, about 10 minutes. Taste; adjust seasonings as necessary.

Makes 4 servings

Rice and Lentil Combo Plate

While visiting Montreal I wandered into a little corner deli that offered an amazing array of hot foods sold by weight. The combination of white rice and lentils was enhanced by a mound of crunchy onions on top. With a side of steamed broccoli, it turned out to be a very satisfying lunch. I put my own twist on this version by using brown rice and a touch of sumac. Be careful not to overcook the lentils or they will become mushy. The instant flour gives the onions an incredible crust.

1½ cups dry lentils
1 bay leaf
2 teaspoons salt, divided
½ teaspoon sumac
3 Tablespoons olive oil, divided
2 yellow onions, divided
1 small carrot, shredded
1 rib celery, minced
2 cups cooked brown rice, at room temperature
Vegetable oil for frying
½ cup instant flour, like Wondra
8 turns of the peppermill
Za'atar (page 16), for serving

Bring the lentils and plenty of water to cover them to a boil. Skim off any froth that rises to the top. Add the bay leaf and 1½ teaspoons of salt; reduce the heat to maintain a strong simmer. Cook for 20 to 25 minutes, until the lentils are tender but not mushy. Remove from heat; drain, return to the pot and season with sumac and 2 Tablespoons of the olive oil.

Meanwhile, heat the remaining Tablespoon of olive oil in a medium skillet over medium heat. Mince 1 of the onions and add to the hot oil with the carrot and celery. Cook about 10 minutes, stirring regularly, until the onions are translucent. Mix the cooked vegetables and rice into the lentils. Set this mixture over low heat to keep warm while you prepare the onion topping.

Just before serving, heat a quarter-inch of vegetable oil in a deep pot until it is very hot but not smoking. While the oil is heating, toss the instant flour, remaining ½ teaspoon salt and the pepper together in a paper bag. Slice the remaining onion in half and cut into ¼-inch lengths between the stem ends; separate into strips. Add the onion strips to the paper bag and shake well to coat them with the seasoned flour. Remove the onions from the bag, shake off any excess flour and carefully drop them into the oil. Stir until crisp and brown (this will likely take 5 minutes or more); remove to paper toweling with a slotted spoon.

To serve, pile the lentil and rice mixture onto a serving plate. Top with the crispy onions and sprinkle with za'atar.

Makes 4 servings

Curried Millet Bowl with Spinach and Garbanzos

Hearty and spicy, these millet bowls are brimming with colorful ingredients that taste great together. Whatever you do, don't skip the chutney. It really makes the dish. Millet, one of our ancient grains, is an excellent pantry item. It stores well and is a delicious, nutrient-rich alternative to rice.

1¼ cups chicken stock
6 sun-dried tomato halves
½ cup millet
1 Tablespoon olive oil, plus 2 teaspoons
1 medium yellow onion, chopped
1 Tablespoon curry powder
1 can (15 ounces) garbanzo beans, rinsed and drained
½ teaspoon salt
1 lemon cut into six wedges
4 cups packed (about 6 ounces) fresh spinach, sliced into ribbons
½ cup prepared mango chutney

Place the chicken stock and dried tomatoes in a heavy saucepan over medium-high heat. Bring to a boil.

Meanwhile, toast the millet; place in a dry skillet and shake over high heat until it is lightly browned and begins to pop. Add the toasted millet to the boiling stock. Reduce the heat, cover and simmer until all liquid is absorbed, about 20 minutes. Remove from heat and allow to stand, still covered, for 10 minutes. Fluff the millet with a fork and remove the tomatoes (don't worry if

SAVORY ASIDE

Major Grey and friends.

Chutney is an Indian condiment generally composed of fruit (or vegetables), spices, a sweetener and vinegar. Some are cooked, others are not. Like mustard, you can make it with a wide variety of ingredients. Perhaps the most common chutney in the United States is mango/ginger, made popular by the famous Major Grey brand. You will find a million recipes for chutney or you can buy it at most supermarkets. Chutney is an indispensible side dish at the Indian table, but also consider it as a condiment for grilled meats and poultry.

some millet sticks to them). When cool enough to handle, chop the tomatoes into smaller pieces. Return to the millet.

Heat the 1 Tablespoon oil over medium heat in a skillet. Add the onion and cook, stirring frequently, until translucent, about 5 minutes. Stir in the curry powder; cook, stirring constantly, for 1 minute. Add the garbanzo beans, millet mixture and salt. Reduce the heat and continue to cook, stirring occasionally, until heated through. Before serving, squeeze in 2 of the lemon wedges.

To serve, line four wide bowls with 1 cup each of the spinach ribbons and drizzle with ½ teaspoon of the remaining olive oil on each serving. Divide the curried millet between the four bowls and top each with 2 Tablespoons of chutney. Garnish with remaining lemon wedges.

Makes 4 servings

Fried Rice

This is a recipe for one serving, maybe two smaller side dish portions. I like it for a quick lunch. For portion control, I transfer the cut veggies to a soup bowl as I prepare them. When the bowl is full, I know I have enough.

---

2 teaspoons olive oil
1 egg
1 cup assorted vegetables cut small to cook quickly (consider carrots, bell peppers, summer squash, cauliflower, broccoli, mushrooms, snow peas or cooked leftover veggies)
¼ cup peas, thawed if frozen
1½ cups cooked long grain rice, cold
1 Tablespoon tamari, plus more for serving
2 green onions, sliced 3 inches into the green part

Heat a wok, wok pan or wide skillet over medium-high heat. Brush with a small amount of olive oil. Crack the egg into the pan, break the yolk and fry until cooked through, turning once. Season with salt and pepper. Transfer the fried egg to a cutting board and cut into small squares.

Return the pan to the heat, add the remaining oil and heat until shimmering. Add the assorted vegetables and peas; cook, stirring almost constantly until the veggies are almost tender, usually less than five minutes. Add the rice and tamari to the pan. Mix well; cook and stir for a few minutes more. Add the chopped egg and sliced green onion. Cook until everything is heated through.

Serve right away with extra tamari sauce, if desired.

Makes 1 serving

Kasha in Acorn Squash Bowls

Here's a meal served in an edible bowl that will please vegetarians and meat eaters alike. Kasha is hefty flakes of buckwheat packed with nutrition. The egg wash at the beginning keeps the grains from becoming mushy. Depending on the size of your squash, you may have some pilaf left over. If so, try it with grated cheese and fried egg for brunch—it's fabulous that way too!

---

2 acorn squash
2 teaspoons olive oil
Salt and freshly milled pepper
1 cup kasha
1 large egg
1 Tablespoon unsalted butter
1 large shallot, minced (about $^1/_3$ cup)
½ teaspoon dill seed
2 cups vegetable stock
¾ cup corn kernels, thawed if frozen
¼ cup dried cranberries
1 teaspoon dried dill weed
1 Tablespoon minced fresh parsley

Preheat the oven to 375 degrees.

Cut each squash in half from stem to blossom end; scrape out the seeds. Brush each half with ½ teaspoon of the olive oil and season with salt and pepper. Place, cut side down, in a large baking dish. Bake for about 45 minutes, or until soft and lightly browned. Leave the oven on while you stuff the squash.

Meanwhile, mix together the kasha and egg in a medium skillet. Turn heat on to medium-high heat and stir the kasha until the egg-coated grains are dry. Remove from heat.

SAVORY ASIDE

Great Grains.

Some people call them superfoods, but I think grains are just a delicious way to add variety to our daily meals. Each different grain, be it kasha or quinoa, barley or millet, requires separate techniques and cooking times, but once you know those, they are almost interchangeable. Add even more variety by varying the cooking liquids and aromatics. Chicken or vegetable stocks impart subtle flavors. Shallots stand in well for onions and/or garlic. The experiments are almost endless when it comes to cooking with these nutritional powerhouses.

Melt the butter in a large saucepan. Add the shallot and dill seed. Sauté for 3 minutes, then stir in the vegetable stock; bring to a boil. Stir in the kasha and return to a boil. Cover, reduce the heat to low and cook for 10 minutes. Add the corn to the pot, return to a boil again; cover and cook 5 minutes more. Stir in the cranberries and dill weed. Remove from heat and let stand, covered for 10 minutes. Stir well, taste for seasonings, adjust as necessary.

Heap the cooked kasha into the cavities of the cooked squash. Bake for 15 minutes, or until heated through. Sprinkle with the fresh parsley and serve right away.

Makes 4 servings

Oven-Baked Falafel

These versatile and spicy falafel patties can be served as is, with the Cucumber Raita (page 135) for dipping or layered into a pita with shredded lettuce and onion slices, as is traditional. You can also make snappy little appetizers by topping the falafel patties with a bit of the raita and some minced tomato, onion and/or avocado. It's no mistake that the garbanzos aren't cooked first. I was surprised to learn that's how it done, but it sure does work.

1 cup dried garbanzo beans
4 teaspoons cumin seeds
4 teaspoons sesame seeds
2 teaspoons coriander seeds
½ teaspoon crushed red pepper
½ cup minced yellow onion
¼ cup olive oil
2 cloves garlic, minced
2 Tablespoons dried parsley
2 teaspoons baking powder
1 ½ teaspoons kosher salt
Non-stick cooking spray
Cucumber Raita, for serving, recipe follows

Soak the beans in plenty of water to cover them overnight.

Combine the cumin seeds, sesame seeds, coriander seeds and crushed red pepper in a small dry skillet over medium high heat. Stirring almost constantly, toast the spices until they are fragrant and you hear a few popping noises. Transfer to a plate to cool.

Drain the soaked beans and place in a food processor fitted with the steel blade. Add the cooled toasted spices, onion, oil, garlic and parsley, baking powder and salt. Whirl everything for quite some time, scraping down the sides repeatedly, to form a smooth consistency.

Preheat the oven to 450 degrees. Spray a baking sheet and your hands with non-stick cooking spray. Form the garbanzo bean mixture into patties that are 2½-inches across and ½-inch thick. Place them on the prepared baking sheet and spray the tops with more non-stick spray. Bake for about 8 minutes; remove from oven and turn the patties over. Bake for 7 minutes more.

Serve warm or at room temperature with Cucumber Raita.

Makes 10

Cucumber Raita

I'm crazy about this refreshing sauce on my curried veggie burgers but it also makes an outstanding garnish for grilled fish or sliced tomatoes.

---

1 medium cucumber
¼ teaspoon salt
½ cup (4 ounces) plain yogurt
1 Tablespoon snipped fresh dill weed (or 1 teaspoon dried)
Zest of a small lemon, minced
Freshly milled black pepper, to taste
Additional salt, if necessary

Peel the cucumber and use a spoon to remove the seeds; shred the flesh into a colander. Toss with the salt and allow to drain for about 15 minutes. Squeeze out as much moisture as possible. Transfer to a small bowl; stir in remaining ingredients. Taste; adjust seasonings as necessary.

Makes about 1 cup

Veggie-Hummus Wrap

Hummus is showing up everywhere these days. It's a great healthy snack that is easy to make but even easier to buy. Here we use a red pepper hummus that always seems to be available next to the others at the market. Various tortilla-like wrappers are also widely available in yummy flavors like spinach or sun-dried tomato; you could use one of those to replace the flour tortilla, if so desired. This is a recipe for a single wrap. Multiply it out if you want more. I like to serve things like this with a little pile of sugar snap peas on the side.

---

1 large (9- or 10-inch) flour tortilla, warmed
$^1/_3$ cup prepared red pepper hummus
¼ cup clover or broccoli sprouts
2 Tablespoons crumbled feta cheese
5 thin slices zucchini
5 thin slices peeled cucumber
3 thin slices from a large ripe tomato

Lay the warmed tortilla out flat and spread the hummus evenly over it to within 2 inches of the edges. Scatter the sprouts over the hummus, pressing down lightly, then do the same with the cheese. Arrange the zucchini slices, slightly overlapping, down the center, again leaving a 2-inch edge. Layer the cucumber and tomatoes over the zucchini.

To wrap and serve, starting at the top and bottom of the lines of veggies, fold in the edges. Next, flip one side of the tortilla over the vegetables and roll into a tight log. Cut the log in half, using a diagonal cut for drama. Serve right away.

Makes 1 serving

Veggie Tacos

One of my favorite lunches, these soft tacos are a terrific way to use up last night's leftover tossed salad. One is usually plenty for me, but the recipe easily expands to make as many tacos you need. Try adding a bit of chopped avocado if you have any on hand.

For each taco:
1 8-inch flour tortilla, warmed
1 Tablespoon sour cream
2 Tablespoons radish, broccoli or alfalfa sprouts
½ cup tossed salad
2 Tablespoons shredded cheddar cheese
1 Tablespoon Quick Fresh Salsa (page 9), or other prepared salsa

Spread the sour cream evenly over one side of the flour tortilla. Scatter the sprouts over sour cream. Place the salad down the center, leaving one inch space near the bottom. Sprinkle the cheese over the salad. Pour the salsa over cheese. Fold up the bottom inch, then fold each side over to make a taco that won't drip.

Makes 1 serving

Ricotta Salad Sandwich

Two lunchtime favorites, the sandwich and a salad, are combined into one here. I like the way the crunch of the veggies gives texture to the creamy cheese while the mustard adds a punch of flavor.

---

2 slices whole wheat bread, toasted
2 teaspoons Dijon mustard
¼ cup ricotta cheese
Salt and freshly milled black pepper, to taste
¼ cup radish, broccoli or alfalfa sprouts
¼ cup thinly sliced, peeled cucumber
3 thin slices from a large ripe tomato
¼ of an avocado, peeled and sliced thin

Spread the mustard, then the ricotta cheese over both pieces of toast evenly; season with salt and pepper. Top one side of the cheese-covered toast with the sprouts, cucumber, tomato and avocado; top with remaining slice of toast. Cut in half on the diagonal and serve immediately.

Makes 1 serving

Garden Vegetable Tomato Sauce

A basket of freshly picked tomatoes inspired this recipe. If you don't want to puree the mixture, just cut the veggies into uniform pieces for even cooking and a nice appearance. Dried herbs will work well—add them when most of the tomatoes have cooked down. This is the perfect sauce for lasagna or other baked casseroles.

---

2 Tablespoons olive oil
1 medium yellow onion, chopped
1 large stalk celery, chopped
1 large carrot, shredded
½ of a large bell pepper, chopped
1 small zucchini, shredded
1 fat clove garlic, minced
4 large (about 2 pounds) ripe tomatoes, cored and chopped (peeled, if desired)
½ teaspoon salt, or to taste
Pinch of sugar
2 Tablespoons fresh oregano leaves
2 Tablespoons fresh basil leaves
2 Tablespoons minced chives
2 teaspoons fresh thyme leaves
Freshly milled black pepper, to taste

Heat the oil over medium-high heat in a large skillet. Add the onion, celery, carrot and bell pepper; cook, stirring regularly, for about 8 minutes or until onion is translucent. Add the zucchini and garlic; cook 2 minutes more. Stir in the tomatoes, salt and sugar. Reduce the heat and cook until the tomatoes have melted and all the veggies are soft. Stir in the herbs and pepper.

If desired, puree the sauce with a hand-held blender or in a food processor. Taste for seasonings. Serve over pasta, grilled eggplant or anything else that strikes your fancy.

Makes about 4 cups

Eggplant Extra

The following recipe is as versatile as it is tasty. Serve it the first time as a side dish, then use leftovers for a zesty pasta sauce adding a bit of crushed red pepper and a healthy grating of Parmesan cheese on top. You might also enjoy it as a pizza topping or on toasted French bread for an easy appetizer. This is what inspired the name; you can always use the extras. It freezes well, too. You may be tempted to skip the salting step but it is necessary to remove bitterness and prevent the eggplant from soaking up all the oil. I tested it both ways and the salting made a far superior sauce.

---

1 medium purple eggplant, peeled if desired and cut into 1-inch cubes
2 teaspoons kosher salt
2 Tablespoons olive oil
1 small yellow onion, chopped
1 cup chopped red and green bell pepper
2 cloves garlic, minced
4-5 Roma tomatoes, chopped
1 teaspoon dried oregano, divided
Salt and freshly milled black pepper, to taste
Small handful of fresh basil torn into small bits
Extra virgin olive oil, for serving, if desired

Place the eggplant cubes in a large colander in the sink. Sprinkle with 1 teaspoon of the kosher salt; toss well and repeat with the remaining teaspoon of salt. Allow the salted eggplant to sit for at least one hour, two is better. Then, transfer the cubes to a double thickness of paper towel and blot the top dry with another paper towel.

Heat the oil in a medium saucepan over medium-high heat. Stir in the drained eggplant and sauté until it softens, about 5 minutes. Stir in the onion and bell pepper; continue cooking and stirring until the onion is wilted, another five minutes. Add the garlic, cook one minute more. Stir in the tomatoes, half of the oregano and a bit of pepper. Reduce the heat to medium, cover and cook until tomatoes have melted, about 10 minutes. Stir in the remaining oregano and the basil. Taste; season with salt and more pepper, if desired.

Serve warm or at room temperature as a side dish garnished with a drizzle of olive oil.

Makes about 4 cups

Taco Stuffed Baked Potatoes, page 156

Vegetables and Side Dishes: Five a day is what they say

Vegetables at the peak of freshness need no embellishment. A dash of salt, perhaps, and a quick grinding of pepper can't hurt. But how often do we actually get that perfect specimen? That's where herbs and spices come in—to enhance the less than exquisite.

In this chapter we use a wide variety of seasonings, both herbs and spices, fresh and dried. You may need to grow some of these highly scented herbs yourself if you hope to enjoy them.

Lemon balm is seldom available as a fresh-cut herb, but you'll find it in the quick to fix and oh-so-tasty Snow Peas with Almonds and Lemon Balm. Put those broccoli stems to use in the equally fast and fresh Broccoli Coins, seasoned with an herbal combination that has subtle hints of lemon. Lemon balm, also known as sweet Melissa, is peasant to grow and a fragrant addition to the garden.

Savory and chervil are other herbs used in this chapter that you may need to grow to enjoy. Both will sprout from seeds in no time. Savory comes in two varieties, summer and winter. The summer type is the annual, and its more tender leaves are better suited to cooking with vegetables. The winter variety (a perennial, so you want to purchase it as a plant) is considered "the bean herb," enhancing beans, of course, but other long-cooking dishes as well.

Chervil is such a pretty little plant you may not want to clip from it, however, the flavor makes this worthwhile. Tasting mildly of licorice combined with pepper, chervil imparts a certain brightness to foods. Try it in an updated classic, Not Your Mother's Peas and Carrots. Garnish this dish with sprigs of chervil in bloom, if possible: The tiny white flowers are enchanting.

Few herbs are as vegetable friendly as dill weed. It goes well with peas, corn, lima beans and carrots, just to name a few. The feathery leaves make a wonderful garnish.

Dill weed is just one of many of the seasonings in Spiced Right Pan-Fried Potatoes. This recipe's savory blend of herbs and spices is punctuated by Hungarian paprika. The combination of dill and paprika is revived again in the fluffy yet crisp Roasted Potato Paprikash.

Dill seed, a product of this annual plant's final stages, offers a more pungent flavor, especially to baked goods or dishes with long cooking times. Try it with cabbage or tomatoes. The seeds complement onion dishes, as well, making a delicious addition to creamed pearl onions or braised leeks.

Potatoes stand up to aggressive seasoning and require more salt than other vegetables. That's why I turn to flavored salts, which I go into greater detail in this chapter.

Saffron, so extravagant and so grand, makes a single appearance here in Saffron Rice Pilaf. Not every spice lover is aware that saffron is the most expensive spice in the world. Saffron is the dried stigma of the purple saffron crocus, a member of the iris family. It blooms for only two or three weeks in autumn. And each step in the cultivation of *Crocus sativus* is accomplished by hand.

Referred to as "strands" in recipes, just about a quarter teaspoon of saffron will season an average dish prepared for four people. Too much saffron turns the pleasant, spicy but bitter flavor into a harsh medicinal taste, so use with caution. It is also lovely in stews or with fish.

Condiments are seasonings, too, and serve us well in flavoring vegetables and side dishes. A splash of sherry vinegar makes a world of difference in heightening the flavors of Skillet Steamed Swiss Chard. For variety and fun, experiment with other vinegars. We all know balsamic vinegar by now, but have you ever used white balsamic? Herbed vinegars, like tarragon or Shiso in a Bottle (page 219), bring the tastes of summer to winter cooking.

I love to use oils to finish a dish. Sesame oil is the star of the show in Sesame Green Beans. Walnut oil gives a gentle undercurrent of flavor while also enhancing the texture of Barley Flakes with Peas.

As you work through these recipes, remember that so many of the herbs and spices are interchangeable. Go with your whims or with what you have hand.

SAVORY ASIDE

Salt to taste.

While these words may seem vague, salt is such a personal seasoning, salting to taste is a good rule of thumb. Too little salt can be corrected at the table in most cases, but if you add too much, it can ruin a dish. It is best to salt in small doses, tasting as you go. It is also important to take the recipe's other ingredients under consideration. Some elements, like Parmesan cheese, mustard or canned goods, bring a salty flavor of their own, so their presence lessens the need for as much salt as you might expect.

Not Your Mother's Peas and Carrots

No squishy carrots or wrinkled-up peas in this fresh take on an excellent, yet often tortured, classic. Chervil is an unusual herb that I encourage you to seek out, however, dill weed would be an acceptable substitute here.

---

3 large carrots, peeled and diced
1 cup fresh peas, or frozen petite
2 Tablespoons unsalted butter, melted
2 Tablespoons minced fresh (or 2 teaspoons dried) chervil, divided
½ teaspoon salt
⅛ teaspoon freshly milled black pepper
Sprigs of fresh chervil, for garnish if desired

Steam the carrots and peas over boiling water for 10 to 15 minutes, until the carrots are tender to your liking. Meanwhile, combine the butter, 1 Tablespoon of the chervil, the salt and pepper in a small bowl. When the carrots and peas are cooked, place into a serving bowl and toss with the seasoned butter. Sprinkle with the remaining chervil. Top with sprigs of chervil, if using, and serve immediately.

Makes 4 servings

Snow Peas with Almonds and Lemon Balm

This fragrant and crunchy side dish goes together in minutes. It's simple to prepare and works well with nearly any main dish.

---

2 Tablespoons sliced almonds
4 ounces fresh snow peas
1 Tablespoon chopped fresh lemon balm leaves
⅛ teaspoon cracked black pepper
⅛ teaspoon kosher salt
1 Tablespoon olive oil

Toast the almonds by placing them in a small dry skillet over medium-high heat. Shake or stir, watching carefully, until they are golden brown. Remove from heat; transfer to a small bowl.

String the snow peas, if desired, and slice crosswise on the diagonal into ½-inch lengths.

After the almonds have cooled, mix in the lemon balm, black pepper and salt, crushing the nuts slightly as you mix.

Heat the olive oil in the same small skillet over medium-high heat. Add the snow pea pieces; stir-fry for 4 to 5 minutes. Reserve 1 Tablespoon of the almond-lemon balm mixture and stir the rest of it into the snow peas. Transfer to a serving dish and sprinkle with the reserved almond mixture.

Makes 2 servings

Broccoli Coins

My friend gave me this idea for using up the broccoli stalks that I usually discard. Just about any fresh herb would work here but the combination below is especially nice. If you want to use dried herbs, add them to the oil/butter combination before the broccoli.

 Stalks only (about 12 ounces) from one head of fresh broccoli
2 teaspoons olive oil
1 teaspoon unsalted butter
2 teaspoons snipped chives
1 teaspoon fresh thyme leaves
1 teaspoon minced lemon balm leaves
Salt and freshly milled black pepper to taste

Use a carrot peeler to remove the tough skin from the broccoli stalks. Slice the stalks into ¼-inch thick rounds.

Heat the oil and butter in a non-stick skillet over medium-high heat. When the oil begins to "ripple," carefully add the broccoli rounds and stir to coat with the oil/butter. Stirring almost constantly, cook about 4 minutes, until the broccoli is tender and beginning to brown. Add the fresh herbs, season with salt and pepper and cook, stirring, another minute.

Makes 4 servings

Skillet Steamed Swiss Chard

It is amazing how a big bunch of chard (or spinach) is reduced to so little after cooking. If you want to make this a meal, try using it as an omelet filling or roll into corn tortillas to make veggie enchiladas.

---

1 large bunch Swiss chard
1 Tablespoon olive oil
2 cloves garlic, peeled and sliced thin
Kosher salt
Freshly milled black pepper
Extra virgin olive oil, for serving
Balsamic vinegar (or try sherry vinegar or tarragon vinegar), for serving

Remove the tough stems from the chard. Wash the leaves well but don't worry about drying them off. Chop the leaves roughly and set aside.

Heat the 1 Tablespoon of olive oil in a wide non-stick skillet over medium-high heat until hot but not smoking. Stir in the garlic and cook, stirring constantly, until fragrant, about 30 seconds. Carefully add the chopped chard with a bit of salt and pepper; toss well. Cover the skillet and allow the chard to steam for a minute or two. Stir and replace the lid, steaming a few minutes more. Season with a bit more salt and pepper before transferring to a serving dish.

Serve warm, passing extra virgin olive oil, balsamic vinegar and a pepper grinder so each diner can dress the chard to personal taste.

Makes 4 servings

Sliced and Braised Fennel

This is a great addition to an antipasto platter or a selection of tapas. I also like to serve it as a green vegetable when Italian dishes are on the menu. Look for the largest fennel bulb you can find; they seem more flavorful than the smaller ones.

---

1 large fennel bulb
1 teaspoon olive oil
1 teaspoon unsalted butter
¼ cup sliced onion
1 clove garlic, sliced
½ teaspoon dried oregano, divided
¼ cup chicken stock
Salt and freshly milled pepper, to taste

To prepare the fennel, cut off the fronds and stalks at the top of the bulb. Mince about 2 teaspoons of the dill-like foliage for a garnish; set aside. Store remaining fronds and stalks for another use. Remove the tough outer layer of the fennel bulb and begin slicing it into thin strips, starting at the top and working your way down to the root end. Stop when you start cutting into the tough root.

Heat the oil and butter in a medium skillet over medium-high heat. Add the sliced fennel and onion. Sauté for 3 to 5 minutes until softened and beginning to brown. Stir often to prevent over-browning. Sprinkle with the sliced garlic and ¼ teaspoon of the oregano. Cook and stir another minute. Pour in the chicken stock; cover and reduce heat to low. Simmer for about 10 minutes, stirring occasionally. Remove the cover, season with the remaining ¼ teaspoon of oregano, salt and pepper. Increase the heat slightly and continue cooking until the liquid has evaporated. Taste; adjust seasonings if necessary. Sprinkle with minced fennel fronds and serve right away.

Makes 4 servings

Sesame Green Beans

I often take this to potluck dinners where the sharp contrast of the deep green beans and the black and white sesame seeds really stands out among all the potato salads and other starchy dishes. It is also a great picnic dish since it is just as good at room temperature as it is hot.

---

1 pound green beans, ends trimmed
2 teaspoons white sesame seeds
2 teaspoons black sesame seeds
1 scant teaspoon kosher salt
¼ teaspoon freshly milled black pepper
1 Tablespoon toasted sesame oil (with chiles, if desired)

Place the beans in a saucepan, cover with water and bring to a boil over high heat. Reduce the heat enough to maintain a strong simmer and cook the beans to your preferred degree of tenderness, from 5 to 20 minutes.

Meanwhile, combine the white and black sesame seeds with the salt and pepper in a small bowl.

After the beans are cooked, drain them and transfer to a serving bowl. Drizzle with the sesame oil and sprinkle with the sesame seed mixture. Toss well. Serve hot or at room temperature.

Makes 4 servings

Cauliflower Gratin

I am crazy about this transformation of plain old cauliflower into something rich and delicious. If you don't have a food processor, simply smash up the cooked cauliflower before combining it with the onions and sour cream.

---

1 head (1½ pounds) cauliflower
4 Tablespoons (½ stick) unsalted butter, divided
1 medium yellow onion, chopped
2 cloves garlic, minced
2 teaspoons sweet paprika
1 cup sour cream
½ teaspoon salt, or to taste
Freshly milled black pepper, if desired
$^2/_3$ cup dry bread crumbs

Core the cauliflower and break it into florets. Steam for about 15 minutes until quite tender.

Meanwhile, melt 3 Tablespoons of the butter in a medium skillet over medium-high heat. Add the onion; cook, stirring regularly, until soft and beginning to brown, about 7 minutes. Stir in the garlic and paprika. Cook another 2 minutes, stirring constantly to prevent the spices from burning. Remove from heat.

Preheat the oven to 350 degrees.

Combine the cooked cauliflower, seasoned onions, sour cream and salt in the bowl of a food processor fitted with the steel blade. Process until nearly smooth. Taste for seasonings, adding more salt and a bit of pepper, if desired. Transfer the cauliflower puree to a buttered 1-quart casserole dish.

In the same skillet that you cooked the onions, melt the remaining Tablespoon of butter. As it melts and becomes fragrant it will take on a browned color from the paprika. Stir in the bread crumbs and cook for a minute or two to crisp them slightly. Spread the bread crumbs over the surface of the cauliflower.

Bake for 25-30 minutes or until the top is browning and the mixture is hot through.

Makes 4 servings

Yellow Squash Sauté

This simple side dish is pretty and delicious. I like to serve it alongside Italian dishes like spaghetti with red sauce or lasagna, although it would work with nearly any meal. To me, zucchini and yellow squash are interchangeable. You could use the green squash, or both, equally as well.

2 Tablespoons olive oil
1 cup thinly sliced red onion
1½ teaspoons dried oregano
4 yellow squash (about 2 pounds), thinly sliced
½ teaspoon kosher salt
Freshly milled black pepper, to taste
¼ cup freshly grated Parmesan cheese

Heat the oil in a wide skillet over medium-high heat. Add the onion, sprinkle with the oregano and stir well. Cook, stirring regularly, for about 5 minutes, or until the onion is softened and just beginning to brown. Add the squash, sprinkle with salt, and continue cooking and stirring for another 5 minutes or so, until the squash is somewhat golden. Transfer to a serving dish and sprinkle with cheese.

Makes 4 to 6 servings

SAVORY ASIDE

Flavored Salts.

Most people are familiar with herbed salts. No spice cabinet is complete without garlic salt, onion salt and celery salt. Unfortunately, these purchased blends are far more salt than flavoring, sometimes as much as 90% salt and 10% garlic, onion or celery seed. Perhaps that is because a producer can sell an inexpensive additive (salt) for the premium price of the seasoning (garlic, etc.). The answer to getting what you pay for is to make your own.

This is done simply by purchasing onion or garlic in "granulated" form (sometimes labeled as powder, but look for the consistency of sugar, not cinnamon) and combining with regular table salt to the proportions of your choosing. Fifty-fifty is a logical place to start, adjusting to satisfy your personal taste. Fill a clean, dry spice jar halfway with granulated garlic or onion, top it off with salt and shake well. For celery salt, which is good in Bloody Marys, use ground celery seed.

Savory Sweets

People seem to really like to make sweet potatoes taste like pumpkin pie. I don't like marshmallows or brown sugar on my vegetables, so I make this savory version. Bear in mind, you may need to add more salt than a recipe calls for if you are using your own new and improved zesty salt blends. The one that follows is written using 50-50 blended salts. Often a point of confusion, sweet potatoes are not yams, but you are welcome to argue with me. I'm referring here to the root vegetable with the gorgeous orange color. You can use plantains, common to Latin cuisines, as well. They are available in many produce sections and resemble a banana's burley country cousin.

SAVORY ASIDE

The veggie plate dinner.

I love to indulge the flexitarian in me with an occasional three-vegetable dinner. With a baked sweet potato at the center, I add a couple of colorful vegetable side dishes. It makes me feel all healthy and virtuous while I still get to enjoy plenty of delicious food.

2 teaspoons garlic salt
2 teaspoons onion salt
1 teaspoon freshly milled black pepper
2 Tablespoons unsalted butter
1 Tablespoon vegetable oil
2 pounds sweet potatoes or firm plantains, peeled and sliced $^1/_8$-inch thick

Combine the garlic salt, onion salt and black pepper in a small bowl.

Melt the butter with the oil in a wide skillet over medium-high heat. Add the sweet potatoes, sprinkle with half the blended salt and pepper. Use a spatula to turn the sweet potatoes, coating with the butter and oil. Fry, stirring frequently, for 10 minutes. Sprinkle with the remaining seasoning mixture and continue cooking until the sweet potatoes begin to brown and are cooked through, about 10 more minutes.

Makes 4 servings

Roasted Potato Paprikash

Crispy on the outside, fluffy on the inside, these spicy potatoes are a terrific complement to a rich main dish. Hot Hungarian paprika gives heat and flavor unlike the often bland paprikas of our childhoods. For a somewhat fire-roasted taste, try smoked Spanish paprika, but add a bit of black pepper too.

1½ pounds Yukon gold potatoes
3 Tablespoons vegetable oil
1½ teaspoons hot Hungarian paprika
1¼ teaspoons salt
¾ teaspoon granulated garlic
¾ teaspoon dried dill weed

Preheat the oven to 450 degrees.

Bring a quart of water to a boil. Peel the potatoes, if desired, and cut into 1-inch chunks. Add to the boiling water and cook for 10 minutes, until softened but still firm. Drain well. Arrange in a baking dish just large enough to hold the potatoes in a single layer.

Combine the oil, paprika, salt, garlic and dill weed. Pour over the potatoes and toss well to coat.

Roast for 10 minutes. Stir the potatoes and roast 10 minutes longer. Sprinkle with additional salt and freshly ground pepper, if desired, and serve hot.

Makes 4 servings

Spiced Right Pan-Fried Potatoes

For a long time I thought of fried potatoes, a staple of my childhood, as fattening. Then it occurred to me, I put practically as much butter on a single baked potato as I use for a whole pan of fried potatoes. Now I'm happy to make them for a big breakfast or a quick dinner side dish.

---

1 Tablespoon dried parsley
1 teaspoon salt
½ teaspoon hot Hungarian paprika
½ teaspoon dried dill weed
¼ teaspoon granulated garlic
¼ teaspoon granulated onion
2 Tablespoons unsalted butter
1 Tablespoon olive oil
3 medium (2 pounds) baking potatoes, peeled

Combine the herbs, salt and spices in a small bowl. (See additional cook's note below.)

Melt the butter with the oil in a heavy skillet over medium-high heat. Carefully slice the potatoes directly into the skillet, cutting random thin pieces. Season with 2 teaspoons of the spice blend. Use a spatula to mix well and stir the potatoes regularly as they begin to brown. After 5 minutes or so, reduce the heat to medium. Continue to cook and stir. When the potatoes are cooked through, season with the remaining spice blend; cook and stir for another minute. Serve hot.

Makes 4 to 6 servings

Cook's note: Another nice way to use this spice blend is for boiled potatoes: Boil new potatoes in plenty of water. When they are cooked, drain off all but 3 Tablespoons of the water. Smash the potatoes with some butter and potato spice.

Taco Stuffed Baked Potatoes

A baked potato as a taco shell, what could be better! It's the perfect food for a Superbowl party or a kids' sleepover. You could serve these as a buffet, letting guests top their own potatoes, or just make them all ahead to let people grab and go.

---

6 large baking potatoes
1 teaspoon ground cumin
1 teaspoon salt
1 recipe (3 cups) Taco Meat Filling, hot (page 99)
1$^1/_3$ cups (6 ounces) shredded Cheddar cheese (a combination of Cheddar and Monterrey Jack is even better)
1 cup Quick Fresh Salsa (page 9)
½ cup sour cream
3 green onions, sliced, including about 1-inch of the green parts

Bake the potatoes in a 400-degree oven for about an hour, or until fork tender.

Meanwhile, combine the cumin and salt. Once the potatoes are out of the oven, use a knife to cut lengthwise into each one. Use a fork to fluff the flesh, divide and sprinkle the cumin/salt mix on the potatoes and fluff again to mix it in. Top each potato with ½ cup of the taco meat, 2 Tablespoons of the cheese, 1 Tablespoon of the salsa, 2 teaspoons of the sour cream and one-sixth of the green onions. Serve right away.

Makes 6 servings

Sunny Pasta Side Dish

Parmesan cheese, not in the green can but a small glass bottle from California, was a real find in Mongolia, where this recipe was created. At home I use fresh Parmesan for an even better taste. The wagon wheel pasta is also nostalgic, since it is what the Mongolian market had. Spirals or bow ties would be perfectly acceptable.

---

2 cups wagon wheel pasta
¼ cup olive oil
3 cloves garlic, minced
¼ to ½ teaspoon crushed red pepper flakes
1 large carrot, finely grated
¼ teaspoon salt
¼ cup grated Parmesan cheese

Cook the pasta according to package directions. Before draining, reserve 1 Tablespoon of the cooking water.

Meanwhile, heat the olive oil over medium heat in a medium saucepan. Add the garlic and red pepper flakes, stirring constantly and being careful not to burn the garlic. After a minute or so, stir in the grated carrot; cook 2 or 3 minutes more, stirring often. Season with salt and keep warm until the pasta is finished cooking.

When the pasta is drained, add to the carrot sauce with the 1 Tablespoon of cooking water. Toss gently but thoroughly to distribute the carrots well. Transfer to a serving dish and sprinkle with the cheese. Serve hot.

Makes 4 side dish servings

Pecan-Cornbread Stuffing

This is my favorite Thanksgiving side dish. The crunchy pecans and cornbread give it a nice bite while the thyme, sage and parsley just sing Thanksgiving. I follow the school of thought that stuffing should not be stuffed. Mostly because I like lots of crispy bits, but I also think stuffing a turkey is a good way to bring food poisoning to the table. Lots of people will disagree, I know. If you choose to stuff, do be sure to remove the stuffing before storing any leftovers.

---

4 Tablespoons (½ stick) unsalted butter
1 medium yellow onion, minced
2 ribs celery, minced
1 Tablespoon fresh thyme, or 1 teaspoon dried
½ teaspoon ground sage
6 cups day-old cornbread broken into chunks (see Mom's Cornbread, page 225—double the recipe and allow to stand uncovered overnight)
¾ cup pecans, toasted and coarsely chopped
¼ cup minced fresh parsley
2 cups chicken or turkey stock, approximately
½ teaspoon salt
⅛ teaspoon freshly milled black pepper, or more to taste

Preheat the oven to 400 degrees.

Melt the butter in a skillet over medium-high heat. Add the onion and celery. Cook, stirring occasionally, about 5 minutes, or until very soft but not browned. Stir in the thyme and sage. Remove from heat; allow to cool slightly.

Meanwhile, place the cornbread, pecans and parsley in a large bowl. Add the cooked onion and celery. Pour in 1½ cups of the stock and stir with a wooden spoon. Add the remaining ½ cup stock if the stuffing seems dry. Add even more if necessary to create a stuffing that is moist but not wet. Stir in the salt and pepper; taste and adjust seasonings as necessary.

Transfer the stuffing to a 9-inch square baking dish. Bake at 400 degrees for about 30 minutes or until the top is beginning to brown and crisp. Can be baked at a lower temperature for longer.

Makes 8 servings

Saffron Rice Pilaf

Delightfully golden and studded with colorful vegetables, this aromatic rice dish feeds all of your senses before you start eating. If you would prefer to use long grain white rice, adjust the cooking time according to the package directions.

---

1 teaspoon unsalted butter
2 teaspoons olive oil
1 cup minced yellow onion
½ cup diced carrots
1 cup long grain brown rice
2 cups hot chicken stock
1 good pinch saffron threads
1 bay leaf
¼ cup petite peas, thawed if frozen
Chopped parsley, for garnish, if desired

In a medium saucepan over medium-high heat, melt the butter with the olive oil. Add the onion and carrots; cook, stirring occasionally, about 5 minutes or until the onions are translucent. Stir in the rice; cook and stir for another 2 minutes. Pour in the hot chicken stock and add the saffron. Bring to a boil, then reduce the heat to a bare simmer. Drop in the bay leaf and add the peas. Cover with a tight-fitting lid and cook for 45 minutes without lifting the lid (or according to rice package directions).

After 45 minutes, check to make sure all the liquid has been absorbed. If it has not, continue cooking for about 5 minutes more. When all the liquid is absorbed, remove from heat and allow to stand, with the lid still on, for 5 minutes. Fluff the pilaf with a fork, remove the bay leaf and transfer the rice mixture to a warmed serving dish. Sprinkle with the chopped parsley, if using, and serve right away.

Makes 6 servings

Spanish Rice

I have tried making restaurant style Spanish rice at home for years without particularly good results. Finally I hit on the perfect combination of flavor and texture while making Crispy Chile Rellenos (page 122). I mention this because I had an extra roasted Anaheim chile that I diced up and tossed in. It turns out this made a real difference. You could use half a small can of roasted green chiles in a pinch. If you prefer white rice over brown, adjust the amount of liquid and the cooking time to match the rice package directions. Don't skip the avocado garnish, it's a marvelous combo!

---

1 Tablespoon unsalted butter
½ cup minced yellow onion
½ cup brown rice
¾ cup chicken stock
½ cup tomato sauce
½ cup peas, thawed if frozen
1 roasted Anaheim chile, peeled, seeded and minced (about 2 Tablespoons)
1 avocado, pitted, peeled and chopped

Melt the butter in a heavy sauce pan over medium-high heat. Add the onion; cook and stir for 5 to 7 minutes or until tender and beginning to brown. Add the rice, stirring to coat with the butter. Pour in the chicken stock and tomato sauce; bring to a boil. Stir well. Reduce heat to a simmer, cover and cook for 50 minutes.

Quickly add the peas and chile pepper to the pot without stirring, return the lid and continue cooking for 10 minutes more. (*Cooking times may vary, check the directions on your rice and adjust as necessary to add the peas and chile pepper 10 minutes before the recommended cooking time.*) Remove from heat; allow rice to stand, covered, for 10 minutes, then fluff with a fork. Serve right away, topping each portion with some of the chopped avocado.

Makes 4 servings

Barley Flakes with Peas and Walnut Oil

By now you may have figured out that peas are my favorite vegetable. If I have overused them, please forgive me. You could replace them here, and in many other recipes, with edamame, lima beans or corn. We talked about barley flakes in the breakfast chapter. Now they make their way to the dinner table. I think this is an extra special substitute for rice with simple broiled chicken or fish.

½ cup frozen petite peas
1 cup barley flakes
2 Tablespoons walnut oil
Zest from 1 small orange
Kosher salt and freshly milled black pepper, to taste
3 green onions, sliced 3 inches into the green parts, for garnish

In a medium saucepan over high heat bring 1 cup of water to a full boil. Add the peas. When the water returns to a boil, stir in the barley flakes. Cover and reduce heat to medium-low. Cook for 5 minutes. Remove from heat and let stand, covered, for 5 minutes.

Fluff the cooked barley flakes with a fork; stir in the walnut oil and orange zest. Add salt and pepper to suit your taste. Transfer to a serving bowl and sprinkle with the green onions. Serve right away.

Makes 4 servings

Composed Tuna Salad, page 179

Salads: On the side or as a meal

You can't go wrong with a salad. Main event or side dish, vegetables in any combination arrive as a welcome addition to the table. Frilly bits of herbs serve to freshen and enliven flavors.

Tender leaves of basil, oregano or parsley straight from the garden will accent the typical leafy greens in your salad bowl. Fronds of dill or a sprinkling of just-plucked thyme leaves give new life to your favorite potato or chopped salad.

Spices and dried herbs also have a place in salads. Paprika will add a jolt of color, seeds add tasty crunch. The possibilities are wide open when it comes to flavor combinations in salad dressings.

Coriander and cumin combined, as in the Corn and Black Bean Salad with Tortilla Strip Croutons, compliment each other well. Their tastes are similar although coriander brings a hint of lemon while cumin offers more earthiness. Epazote, the bean herb, adds depth to all the flavors of the salad, tying it all together.

You may need to grow epazote if you want to use it fresh, although it is starting to become mainstream. This tough herb from Mexico has spiked, serrated leaves that some folks say don't smell very good.

Throughout these recipes you will see representatives of the onion family. Petite chives give color and just a nip of flavor to the Egg and Tuna Roll-Ups. Chive flowers, when available, make a gorgeous garnish if left whole but are overpowering for eating. That's why we mince them into the Egg Salad with Walnut Oil. If you grow nothing else, you should have a pot of chives. They will produce year-round in a sunny windowsill and thrive on being snipped. Harvest entire leaves by clipping from the base of the plant to encourage more growth.

A close cousin to chives, the green onion is attractive in salads and palatable enough to eat raw. They make a good base for the Gazpacho Salad and a serve as a colorful textural counterpart in the Wild Rice Salad. Green onions are often added to a recipe in two parts. The white portion is introduced while cooking or mixing. The sliced green ends serve as a flavorful garnish later.

Shallots are the near perfect onion for a salad dressing or sauce, providing the combined tastes of onion and garlic without a major presence. Shallots look like garlic but peel like an onion. They make an acceptable, yet milder, substitute for either one.

Although I usually preach about the taste superiority of making your own foods, good things can and do come from a bottle or jar. Roasted red peppers are an excellent example of this. Not that you can't roast them yourself (see page 221), but fresh red bell peppers are sometimes expensive or not available. Open a jar and you can add instant color to a dish as on the Composed Tuna Salad plate.

Prepared salad dressings are often unsatisfying, but there are good ones out there that are worth keeping on hand for an easy finish. I have gotten rave reviews for a simple salad of packaged cole slaw mix tossed with ranch dressing and a few twists of black pepper. A substantial salad is never far away if you keep the ingredients for the Quick Garbanzo Toss on hand. Fresh spinach is a worthy substitute if you aren't growing arugula.

Gardeners of every skill set should investigate growing arugula. It does well in pots, has a short growing time and is one of those leafy greens that are referred to as "cut and come again." This means you can snip all you want and it will grow more. I love the nutty sharpness that arugula, also known as rocket or rucola and other names, brings to sandwiches and salads. Try it as a pizza topping once the pie comes out of the oven or stuff it into omelets just before serving.

This chapter also has hearty salads that are suitable to serving as a main dish. A Taco Salad Buffet gets you out of the kitchen to visit with guests while allowing them to have some fun creating a meal that is spiced to their own taste. The Basic Chicken Salad, aromatic with tarragon, is always a big hit whether it is served as a sandwich filling or piled onto greens.

Tarragon is a faithful garden plant, returning year after year in all but the coldest climates. It is often considered an inferior dried herb, but I've noticed that leaves I dry myself seem more flavorful than those bought in jars. Flavored vinegar is a terrific way to preserve the fresh taste of tarragon throughout the winter.

Although we often associate them with light, summer eating, salads are yummy year round. They adapt well to the changing seasons; whatever is fresh is the perfect ingredient. Be flexible and creative and you'll never eat the same salad twice.

Corn and Black Bean Salad with Tortilla Strip Croutons

If you can get fresh corn, chiles and epazote, by all means use them: Steam 2 ears of corn in their husks for 3 minutes in the microwave on high. Roast a poblano or Anaheim chile, peel, seed and chop. Use 3 teaspoons minced fresh epazote. For maximum flavor, make this salad the day before. Store in the refrigerator and bring to room temperature before serving. This colorful salad also works as a hearty salsa.

---

2 cups frozen corn kernels, cooked according to package directions and drained
1 can (15 ounces) black beans, rinsed and drained
1 can (4.5 ounces) diced green chiles
1 large clove garlic, minced
1 medium tomato, cored and diced
1 teaspoon ground coriander
3 Tablespoons olive oil
5 teaspoons red wine vinegar
1½ teaspoons finely chopped dried epazote
½ teaspoon kosher salt
⅛ teaspoon freshly milled black pepper
Tortilla Strip Croutons, recipe follows

Place the corn, black beans, green chiles, garlic and tomato into a large salad bowl. Sprinkle with the coriander and toss well.

Whisk together the oil, vinegar, epazote, salt and pepper; pour over the corn and bean mixture. Toss well. If time permits, cover and place in refrigerator overnight. Bring to room temperature before serving.

To serve, mound on a salad plate and scatter the Tortilla Strip Croutons over the top.

Makes six ½ cup servings

Tortilla Strip Croutons

6 six-inch corn tortillas
Vegetable oil for frying
1 teaspoon salt
1 teaspoon ground cumin

Cut the tortillas in half, stack and slice into half-inch strips. Heat ½ inch of oil in a deep, heavy saucepan over medium-high heat. The oil is ready when a test tortilla strip dipped into it sizzles heartily.

Carefully drop about one-third of the strips into the hot oil; keep them moving with a slotted spoon and fry until crisp, about 4 minutes. Carefully transfer to layers of paper towels to drain. Repeat two more times with remaining tortilla strips.

Mix together the salt and ground cumin. Sprinkle this mixture over the warm tortilla strips and toss lightly to coat.

Makes about 1 cup

Gazpacho Salad

For an impressive presentation, as well as a heartier dish, arrange this refreshing salad over half a peeled avocado on a lettuce-lined salad plate.

Dice each of the following uniformly small:
1 small bunch green onions, with most of green parts
3 Roma tomatoes, cored
2 ribs celery
1 large carrot, peeled
1 cucumber, peeled and seeded
1 green bell pepper, cored

For the dressing:
¼ cup tomato juice
1½ Tablespoons fresh lemon juice
1½ Tablespoons olive oil
2 teaspoons minced garlic
½ teaspoon dried basil
½ teaspoon salt
⅛ teaspoon freshly milled black pepper

For the garnish:
6 large lettuce leaves
¼ cup chopped parsley

Toss the diced vegetables together in a large bowl.

Combine the dressing ingredients in a small jar with a lid; shake well. Pour dressing over vegetables; toss well. Chill.

To serve, line a platter with the lettuce leaves. Heap the salad onto the lettuce and sprinkle with parsley.

Makes 8 cups or 6 to 8 servings

SAVORY ASIDE

Citrus Supreme.

To "supreme" an orange, or any citrus fruit, slice off the stem end and also the opposite end. Set one of these flat sides down on a cutting board. Use a serrated knife to remove the peel from top to bottom by following the line between the flesh and the skin all around the fruit. Working over a bowl to catch the juices, carefully cut out each segment by running the knife between the flesh and the white membranes. These peeled segments are called a supreme.

Arugula and Orange Salad

Salads don't get much prettier than this one. With all the bright colors and bold flavors, it is nice to serve alongside a hearty winter meal.

---

    4 cups torn arugula leaves
    ½ teaspoon kosher salt
    ⅛ teaspoon freshly milled black pepper, or to taste
    2 oranges, supremed
    ¼ cup Tarragon-Walnut Vinaigrette, recipe follows
    ¼ cup chopped toasted walnuts

Place the arugula leaves into a salad bowl and sprinkle with the salt and pepper. Toss well. Drop the orange segments into the bowl, drizzle on the vinaigrette; toss again. Sprinkle the salad with the walnuts. Serve immediately.

Makes 4 servings

Tarragon-Walnut Vinaigrette

This dressing is especially delectable on a simple salad of assorted fresh greens. Add a sliced pear, Gorgonzola cheese and a scattering of toasted walnuts to create a popular salad.

---

3 Tablespoons walnut oil
1 Tablespoon minced shallot
2 Tablespoons champagne vinegar
1 teaspoon chopped fresh tarragon (a 6-inch sprig)
(or use 2 Tablespoons tarragon vinegar instead of the vinegar and tarragon)
½ teaspoon Dijon mustard
Pinch of kosher salt
3 turns of peppermill, or to taste

Combine all ingredients in a small jar with a tight fitting lid. Shake well.

Makes about ⅓ cup

SAVORY ASIDE

Nut oils.

Walnut oil is my secret weapon when it comes to salads. With such a rich flavor, it gives a salad dressing extra punch as well as a terrific texture. Other oils are interesting to play with for the broad range of flavors. Sesame oil is so appealing in a toasty, nutty way. I like to use hazelnut oil, too, as it is locally produced where I live.

Wild Rice Salad

I like the cooked rice to retain a toothsome bite for this salad so I start checking the texture about 10 minutes before the package's directions suggest as the minimum cooking time. This salad keeps well covered in the refrigerator but bring it to room temperature before serving. You could also serve it hot as a pilaf.

---

1 cup wild rice
1 cup fresh or frozen peas
⅓ cup Tarragon-Walnut Vinaigrette (page 170)
1 large carrot, shredded (about 1 heaping cup)
1 stalk celery, thinly sliced (about ¾ cup)
3 green onions, sliced 3 inches into the green parts
Salt and freshly milled pepper, to taste

Cook the wild rice according to package directions. Place the peas into a colander. When the rice is finished cooking, drain it into the colander over the peas to cook them slightly. Allow the rice to cool for about 10 minutes. Transfer to a serving bowl and toss with the vinaigrette. Stir in the carrot, celery and green onions. Season with salt and pepper to taste. Serve right away.

Makes about 6 cups or 6 to 8 servings

Quick Garbanzo Toss

This is another one of my go-to potluck or picnic recipes. It is easy to double and takes just a few minutes to put together. I always use ranch dressing, but I'll bet a Caesar would be tasty, too.

1 can (15 ounces) garbanzo beans, drained and rinsed
½ cup roasted red pepper strips, drained on paper toweling
1 cup packed arugula leaves, torn into bits if large
¼ cup creamy bottled dressing, more or less to taste
Plenty of freshly ground black pepper

Combine all the ingredients and serve at room temperature.

Makes 2 to 4 servings

SAVORY ASIDE

First you make a salad.

You can pay top dollar for a bag of salad already prepared in the produce department of your local supermarket. Or, you can put together your own convenience food that's fresher and will last longer. I often offer it as a tossed salad at dinner and put the extras into a plastic bag for later use. Squeeze as much air out of the bag as possible before closing with a twist tie. If you want to make it ahead, mix it right in the bag. Here are the basics: 2 cups *each* torn spinach, Romaine lettuce and red leaf lettuce; 1 cup sliced cucumber (or zucchini) half moons; 1 cup shredded carrots; ½ cup red bell pepper strips (1x¼-inch); ½ cup sliced celery; ¼ cup sliced green onion; and 2 thinly sliced radishes. This will give you nine cups of colorful salad. Use this for any of these green salads or as a filling for Veggie Tacos (page 137).

Taco Salad Buffet

While this is a great buffet meal, you could also prepare individual plates to serve to guests. Start with a ring of tortilla chips around the edge of a large dinner plate then heap on the salad. Scatter the tomatoes and olives over the lettuce mix, top with a scoop of taco meat and surround that with a circle of kidney beans. Garnish the salad with a sprinkling of cheese, a scoop of guacamole and a scoop of sour cream. For presentation purposes, pass the dressing on the side so everyone can see how pretty the salad is.

For the salad:
2 cups *each* torn spinach, Romaine lettuce and red leaf lettuce
1 cup sliced cucumber
1 cup shredded carrots
½ cup sliced celery
¼ cup sliced green onion

For the buffet:
1 recipe Taco Meat Filling, warmed (page 99)
1 bag (10 ounces) corn tortilla chips
1 can (15 ounces) kidney beans, rinsed and drained
1 large tomato, chopped
1½ cups (6 ounces) shredded cheese, half cheddar, half Monterrey Jack
¾ cup sliced black olives
¼ cup sliced pickled jalapenos
1 cup sour cream
2 cups guacamole
1½ cups Quick Fresh Salsa (page 9)
1 recipe Taco Salad Dressing, recipe follows
Additional salad dressings, if desired

Toss together the ingredients for the salad. Chill while preparing the buffet.

To set the buffet, arrange serving plates at one end of the table. Place the tortilla chips before the salad mix, encouraging guests to build their salads on a bed of chips. Arrange the other buffet items attractively down the table, ending with the sour cream, guacamole and salad dressings.

Makes a buffet for 6

Taco Salad Dressing: Mix together ½ cup *each* salsa and sour cream with a dash of ground cumin until well blended.

Old-Fashioned Ham Salad

I'm crazy about this as a simple sandwich filling. It is as good on a fluffy potato roll as it is on the firm Salt and Pepper Rolls on page 64. You could also use it to fill endive cups over a bed of shredded lettuce or as a spread for crackers.

---

8 ounces cooked ham, preferably Black Forest, cut into large cubes
¼ cup mayonnaise
2 Tablespoons dill pickle relish (or use chopped dill pickles)
1 Tablespoon Dijon-style mustard
1 Tablespoon snipped chives
1 teaspoon dried chervil (or parsley, if you must)
Freshly milled black pepper, to taste

In a food processor fitted with the steel blade, chop the ham fine. Add the mayonnaise, relish and mustard. Process to the consistency of a spread, scraping down the sides a couple of times to mix well. Add the chives, chervil and black pepper, pulse to combine, again scraping down the sides of the bowl. Taste and adjust seasonings as necessary to suit your taste.

Makes 1½ cups

Basic Chicken Salad

I call this basic because you can add a variety of ingredients to give it a new twist each time you prepare it. You might want to toss in a handful of toasted nuts or dried fruit like cherries or cranberries. Substitute rosemary or curry powder for the tarragon to give a different, yet equally delicious, flavor. This recipe involves poaching raw chicken. If you are using chicken that is already cooked you'll just need to combine all the ingredients.

2 cups water
5 whole peppercorns
1 bay leaf
2 four-inch sprigs fresh tarragon
1 pound boneless, skinless chicken breasts
3 ribs celery, minced
5 green onions, sliced with about 4 inches of the green parts
1 large carrot, shredded
2/3 cup mayonnaise
2 Tablespoons grainy mustard
1 teaspoon dried tarragon (or 1 Tablespoon fresh)
Salt and freshly milled pepper to taste

In a skillet over high heat, bring the water, peppercorns, bay leaf and tarragon to a boil. Reduce the heat to maintain a bare simmer. Place the chicken into the water. The chicken should be about halfway immersed, add more or remove some as necessary. Cover and poach by keeping the water just barely at a simmer until the chicken is cooked through, 10 to15 minutes, depending on thickness of chicken pieces, turning once. Remove from the water to cool. (Discard this water or use for chicken stock in another recipe.)

When cool enough to handle, shred the chicken or cut into bite-size pieces. Place in a large bowl and add remaining ingredients. Mix well. Chill, if desired.

Makes about 3 cups

One of my favorite things to make when I'm going to have a group of girlfriends over for lunch is a three salad plate. Usually this includes ham salad, chicken salad and either egg or tuna salad, maybe the two combined. Start with a lettuce leaf-lined plate, add some chopped lettuce then top with a scoop of each salad. Add a few carrot sticks, sugar snap peas and fresh red pepper strips on the side. Crisp crackers or warm bread make the perfect accompaniment. Don't forget to serve a chilled sparkling wine and decadent dessert.

Stuffed Avocado Salad

This is a showy yet easy brunch dish that adapts to any whim. Stuff the avocado with tuna or shrimp salad instead of chicken. Consider other garnishes like grapes, radishes or freshly snipped chives. For croissants you can always substitute a fan of assorted crackers or a pair of crossed breadsticks.

---

6 cups mixed salad greens, cleaned, washed and torn into pieces
2 ripe avocados, halved and pitted
3 cups Basic Chicken Salad (page 175)
8 tomato wedges
½ cup sprouts, like alfalfa, radish or broccoli
16 thinly sliced red onion rings
4 warmed croissants, if desired

Divide the salad greens between four chilled plates. Using a large spoon, carefully remove the flesh from each avocado half in one piece. Place each half, pitted side up, in the center of the greens on the plate. Fill each avocado cavity with ¾ cup of the chicken salad, allowing it to spill over the sides as necessary. Arrange 2 tomato wedges, 2 Tablespoons of the sprouts and 4 red onion slices decoratively around each of the avocados. Add a croissant to each plate, if using. Serve immediately.

Makes 4 servings

Egg and Tuna Roll-Ups

When I was a kid my mom made large quantities of egg salad so we could all have sandwiches. She always used a pastry blender to chop up the eggs. I thought that was the tool's main function until I became a well-rounded cook much later. Wraps are popular these days, so this tasty sandwich fits right in. For extra color, consider spinach or red pepper wraps, available at most supermarkets, to replace the wheat flour tortillas.

---

2 hard-boiled eggs, peeled
1 can (6 ounces) tuna, drained
2 Tablespoons mayonnaise
1 Tablespoon dill relish (or minced dill pickle)
1 Tablespoon snipped chives
2 teaspoons minced fresh savory (or whatever fresh herb you have on hand)
Salt and freshly milled black pepper, to taste
2 eight-inch whole wheat flour tortillas
¼ cup sprouts, like alfalfa, radish or broccoli

Place the eggs into a small bowl and use a fork (or pastry blender) to break them into coarse bits. Stir in the tuna, mayonnaise, relish, herbs, salt and pepper. Mix well to combine.

To roll into wraps, heat a large non-stick griddle (or skillet) over medium-high heat. Warm the tortillas on both sides. Transfer to plates. Divide the salad mixture between the two tortillas, spreading it evenly to about ½-inch from the edges. Top with 2 Tablespoons of the sprouts. Tuck in the ends and roll into a wrap. Cut in half on the diagonal and serve.

Makes 2 servings

Egg Salad with Walnut Oil

This is an unusual take on egg salad. Serve it on crackers as an appetizer or with a bowl of soup at lunchtime. Pretty purple flowers are an occasional gift from your herb garden's tuft of chives. They serve as a gorgeous garnish, but be warned: they pack an intense onion punch when consumed whole. Did you know that eggs that are less than fresh are easier to peel once they are boiled?

---

4 hard-boiled eggs, peeled
3 small chive blossoms, if available, or 2 teaspoons snipped chives
2 Tablespoons walnut oil
1 Tablespoon minced fresh dill weed (or use 1 teaspoon dried)
Salt and freshly milled black pepper, to taste

Place the eggs in a small bowl and use a fork (or a pastry blender) to break them up into coarse bits. Mince one of the chive flowers and mix into the eggs with the walnut oil and dill; season with the salt and pepper. Serve on toast or crackers, if desired, garnishing the dish with the remaining chive flowers.

Makes 1½ cups

Composed Tuna Salad

This is a wonderful salad to make in the dead of winter since most of the ingredients come from the pantry. A really good tuna from Italy or Spain is a must here. The fresh tarragon and parsley certainly enhance the salad greens but don't worry if they aren't available, it will still be full of flavor.

---

4 cups torn leaf lettuce
4 cups torn romaine lettuce
1 small carrot, shredded
½ of a zucchini (or cucumber), quartered and sliced
4 green onions, sliced, white and green parts kept separate
2 Tablespoons chopped fresh flat-leaf parsley, if available
1 Tablespoon chopped fresh tarragon leaves, if available
¼ teaspoon kosher salt
4 cans (5 ounces each) best-quality tuna in olive oil, undrained
1 cup sliced black olives
2 cans (15 ounces each) white beans, rinsed and drained
1 cup roasted red bell pepper strips
2 Tablespoons tarragon vinegar
Freshly milled black pepper

Make a tossed salad with the lettuces, carrots, zucchini and the white parts of the green onions. Sprinkle with the fresh herbs, if using, and the salt; toss again. Divide the salad mix among 4 dinner plates.

Drain the oil from the cans of tuna into a small bowl to use as part of the dressing. Arrange the tuna in a strip down the center of the salad on the plates. In two strips on either side of the tuna, arrange 2 Tablespoons of the black olives. Next to the olives on both sides of each plate, make two more strips with 1/4 cup of the beans. Finish each plate with 2 Tablespoons of the red pepper strips on either side of the beans.

To dress the salads, drizzle the reserved tuna juice over the ingredients, especially the beans. Sprinkle each plate with 2 teaspoons of the tarragon vinegar. Finish with a grinding of pepper and sprinkling of the green onion tops.

Makes 4 servings

Papaya-Shrimp Salad

Make this salad with only the freshest, most perfect ingredients. I suggest tiny bay shrimp because where I live we can often get them fresh, but any seafood, even a simple fillet of fish, would work just as well. Think of herbs like tarragon, chives, basil, parsley and thyme for tossing into the lettuce. By using a wide variety of herbs you offer an amazing flavor contrast with each bite. Mint is especially terrific here. The papaya seeds provide a peppery bite. Pass the pepper mill at the table in case your guests wish to add more.

---

1 small head of butter lettuce, torn into bite-size pieces
1 cup loosely packed coarsely chopped fresh mixed herbs
1 pound bay shrimp, cooked and shelled
½ cup papaya seed dressing or other creamy-style salad dressing of your choice
1 papaya, peeled, halved, seeded and sliced ½-inch thick, reserving 3 Tablespoons of the seeds
1 small cucumber, peeled and sliced ½-inch thick
1 avocado, sliced
1 large tomato, cored and cut into wedges
2 boiled eggs, peeled, halved and cut into wedges

Toss the lettuce with the fresh herbs and divide evenly between four dinner plates, covering the entire plate to make a bed for the remaining ingredients. Mound one quarter of the shrimp onto the center of each bed of lettuce. Use two Tablespoons of the salad dressing for each plate, drizzling it in a circle surrounding the base of the shrimp mound. Sprinkle about two teaspoons of papaya seeds over each of the plates making sure a few land on top of the shrimp mound to provide a striking contrast.

Cut the halved and sliced papaya again lengthwise and arrange one quarter of the slices in a fan around one area of the shrimp (thinking of it like a clock, cover the area of 1 to 4). Continue fanning out groups of the remaining ingredients in the same clock-like pattern to completely surround the mounds of shrimp on each plate.

Makes 4 servings

Congo Bars, page 189

Sweets: Sometimes you need a little something

Ah sweets, creamy and dreamy or crisp and crackly, we love them all. The following dessert recipes run the gamut from small treats to exotic concoctions, each with an unusual twist to surprise and delight.

Few of the dessert spices can be grown in the typical garden. Allspice, ginger, nutmeg and cloves, cinnamon and vanilla, these all come from tropical locations and require specialized processing.

To garner the most intense flavors from these spices, try to buy them whole and grind them yourself. A coffee grinder devoted to spices is the best choice, but you can also use a mortar and pestle. Tiny graters are available for nutmeg, which really should be freshly ground.

The dessert herbs, however, can be grown by even the novice gardener. Rosemary will flourish year after year in any climate with a bit of tender, loving care. Mint, in its many varieties, will literally take over a garden if left unchecked. Fragrant lavender is finicky to climate and conditions but will reward all of the senses with its blooms.

In the recent past, few cooks considered lavender a culinary herb, given its many uses in crafts and aromatherapy. That is changing these days. Adventurous chefs are using the lovely flower buds in dishes sweet and savory. Do make sure that the lavender you purchase for cooking is of "culinary grade."

Lavender can be overpowering when used with a heavy hand so start slowly to familiarize yourself with it. The pleasant, flowery balsam taste will turn astringent if too much is added to a dish. Often just a teaspoon will be enough for a basic recipe.

Lavender Sugar is a good jumping off point for new culinary adventures if you are unfamiliar with the herb. As exemplified in Fresh Fruit and Lavender Parfaits, where Lavender Sugar sweetens the whipping cream, this flavored sugar can be used as a substitute for regular sugar in many recipes. Try it in lemonade or sugar cookies, over fresh berries or with a cup of tea.

Fresh rosemary in desserts often creates an interesting surprise. I first learned this from *The Joy of Coffee,* by Corby Kummer. He uses the dried herb in his Rosemary Zaletti, one of my favorite cookies. Here, fresh minced rosemary is combined with dried lavender for Rosemary-Lavender Brownies.

The all-American favorite dessert takes another unusual twist in Mint Pesto Brownies. Garden-fresh mint leaves are transformed into a paste with macadamia nuts, honey and vanilla, then swirled through a brownie batter. People who taste these are puzzled at first, but are soon reaching for more.

The same is true with Cacao Nib-Orange Crepes. This dazzling and delicious dessert is perfect for the end of a lighter meal. These crepes are filled with ricotta cheese and topped with sautéed oranges. The surprise comes with the cacoa nibs, ground into the crepes and sprinkled over top as a garnish.

Cacao nibs are also a recent introduction into the mainstream culinary world. Nibs are little bits of raw, unsweetened chocolate, perfect for spiking desserts and not a bad snack either. They add a chocolaty crunch to the Congo Bars, as well.

Not all sweets need to be high calorie indulgences. Light Vanilla Cake keeps the texture of traditional cake without all the fat and cholesterol. It is a terrific starting point for an unlimited number of dessert combinations.

The Summer Fruit Crisp has a tasty, crunchy topping that works on any fruit, year-round. With four tablespoons of butter for eight servings, it falls into the healthy dessert category.

The true flavors of dessert for those long cold winters are allspice, nutmeg, ginger and cinnamon. My Best Pumpkin Pie is a favorite at Thanksgiving. Spicy Pumpkin Squares are homey enough for everyday meals, but rich enough for special occasions, too.

Nearly every dessert recipe calls for vanilla. This delicate flavor has a tendency to make foods taste more like themselves. Use only high-quality extract. While it is more expensive than imitation vanilla flavorings, the cost difference is credited to what you don't get. Artificial vanillas are frequently made from vanillin, a by-product of wood pulp production or other processes that do not appeal to my taste buds.

The vanilla bean is an exquisite spice. Also pricey, it is worthy of a splurge at least every now and then. Use a whole bean when you want the true taste of vanilla to shine through. To use one, carefully cut it in half lengthwise. Run the blade of a sharp knife down the inside, scraping out the fleshy pulp. Add this and the scraped bean to the liquid in your recipe. Ideally, you would allow this to steep for 15 to 20 minutes. Remove the seeded bean before serving or mixing with other ingredients.

To get a bit more mileage from a bean after cooking with it, rinse and dry, then sink the halves into your sugar bowl. After a couple of weeks you will have a pleasant vanilla sugar for baking or sweetening coffee and tea. Or you might try chopping up the used bean and tossing it in with coffee before brewing a pot.

Sesame has long been used in cookies or sweetened bars, particularly in Asian cultures. Sesame Seed Ice Cream was inspired by a dessert at a Japanese restaurant in Korea. The toasted tahini called for in the recipe is available in jars at most supermarkets and health food stores. Tahini is an unsweetened sesame seed paste that shouldn't be confused with sesame butter, also available. Common to Middle Eastern recipes like hummus and baba gahnouj, tahini also makes an excellent shortbread called halvah.

A sprig of fresh mint leaves is the typical dessert plate garnish. Attractive as this may be, with a bit of creativity you can come up with more appropriate and original finishes.

Start by considering the ingredients of the dish. With the Cacao Nib-Orange Crepes, the sprinkling of nibs over the orange sauce gives your guests a clue about the flavors on the plate. Dashes of freshly grated nutmeg hint at more warming tastes to come, while a dusting of cocoa indicates chocolate in the dish.

Edible flowers, candied or left plain, are a gorgeous garnish for fruit desserts. A pair of crossed cinnamon sticks or other whole spices are not really meant to be eaten but do create a spectacular effect in a large dessert presentation.

As with all the courses of your meal, be it for two or 20, make the dessert special. These recipes will get you started. As you will see, they all leave plenty of room for experimentation and substitutions so that you can stamp them with a signature that is all your own.

Summer Fruit Crisp

Every kitchen should have a nutmeg grater. They come in a variety of styles from very basic to elaborate. Most fruits would work in this recipe. You could even use a canned pie filling in a pinch. It is the topping with which I fell in love. Peeling the fruit is optional; it is a nice quick recipe for the family if you choose not to, but more elegant if you do peel them.

---

²/₃ cup rolled oats
⅓ cup packed brown sugar
⅓ cup whole wheat flour
⅓ cup sliced almonds
½ teaspoon freshly grated nutmeg
4 Tablespoons (½ stick) unsalted butter, chilled and sliced
5 cups fresh fruit such as sliced peaches, apricots and blueberries
3 Tablespoons sugar, more or less to taste, depending on sweetness of fruit
1 Tablespoon vanilla extract
½ teaspoon ground cinnamon
½ cup heavy cream, optional

Preheat the oven to 375 degrees. Butter an 8-inch baking dish, or coat it with non-stick spray.

In a medium mixing bowl, combine the oats, brown sugar, whole wheat flour, almonds and nutmeg. Add the sliced butter, working it in with your fingertips until you get a mixture of crumbs the size of peas or smaller.

In another mixing bowl, combine the fruit with the sugar, vanilla and cinnamon. Toss lightly but well to coat the fruit evenly. Transfer to the prepared pan. Sprinkle the topping mixture evenly over the fruit.

Bake for about 30 minutes, or until the topping begins to brown and the filling is bubbly.

Drizzle each serving with the heavy cream, if desired.

Makes 6 to 8 servings

Light Vanilla Cake

This versatile vanilla cake recipe is lightened up by reducing the traditional amount of butter and by using just the whites of the eggs. Buttermilk gives us a more tender cake. Use a whole vanilla bean to add extra depth of flavor. Think of this cake as a base for a wide variety of desserts. You could split it into two layers for a traditional cake with frosting, fill it with jam and sprinkle the top with powdered sugar, or serve it with ice cream or frozen yogurt and chocolate sauce. It's great with fresh or canned berries.

1½ cups cake flour
1 teaspoon baking powder
¼ teaspoon baking soda
¼ teaspoon salt
3 Tablespoons unsalted butter, softened
¾ cup sugar
2 large egg whites
2 teaspoons vanilla extract
¾ cup buttermilk

Preheat the oven to 350 degrees. Grease and flour an 8-inch square baking pan.

Combine the flour, baking powder, baking soda and salt; set aside. In a medium bowl with an electric mixer, cream the butter and sugar until light and fluffy. This may take several minutes because of the reduced amount of butter. Mix in the egg whites and vanilla. Add half of the flour mixture; beat well. Pour in all of the buttermilk; beat well. Scrape down the sides of the bowl and add the remaining flour; beating well again. Pour the batter into the prepared pan, smooth the top and bake for 30 to 35 minutes, or until a toothpick inserted in the center comes out clean.

Makes 6 to 8 servings (or more, depending on how you serve the cake)

Rosemary-Lavender Brownies

Here's a recipe I developed when someone wrote to my website wondering if I had a recipe for brownies with rosemary and lavender. I love to see the look on a person's face when they try these for the first time. They just can't figure out what makes them so delicious.

---

4 squares (4 ounces) unsweetened chocolate
¾ cup (1½ sticks) unsalted butter
2 cups sugar
3 large eggs
2 teaspoons vanilla extract
½ cup all-purpose flour
½ cup whole wheat pastry flour
1½ teaspoons minced fresh rosemary
1 teaspoon dried lavender flowers, crushed

Preheat the oven to 350 degrees. Line a 13x9-inch baking pan with foil; coat the foil with non-stick spray.

Melt the chocolate with the butter (2 minutes on high, if using a microwave). When the chocolate is completely melted, stir in the sugar. Add the eggs and vanilla, mixing well. Stir in the flours, rosemary and lavender until well blended.

Spread in the prepared pan. Bake until the brownies begin to pull away from the edges of the pan and the center is set, 30 to 35 minutes. Be careful not to overbake or they will be dry. Cool on a rack in the pan and then lift out the foil before cutting into bars.

Makes 16 to 24 brownies, depending on how you cut them

SAVORY ASIDE

Mint Mania.

With so many great ways to use mint, from drinks and salads to desserts and garnishes, it makes sense to grow your own. You might want to try more than one variety. Spearmint is the most common for cooking, but peppermint is good for desserts and tea. It is best to grow mint in a pot, even one buried in the ground, because mint is an aggressive spreader. It will tolerate full sun but does best in partial shade.

Mint Pesto Brownies

To swirl the pesto into the brownies, try placing the pesto in a small plastic bag with a corner snipped off. Pipe lines of pesto going one direction and run a knife through the lines in the opposite direction to swirl.

---

6 Tablespoons (¾ stick) unsalted butter
2 squares (2 ounces) unsweetened baking chocolate
1 cup sugar
2 large eggs
1 teaspoon vanilla extract
½ cup all-purpose flour
¼ cup Mint Pesto (page 215)

Preheat the oven to 350 degrees. Lightly butter an 8-inch square baking pan, or coat it with non-stick spray.

Melt the butter and chocolate together until smooth (1 minute on high, if using a microwave). When the chocolate is completely melted, stir in the sugar. Beat in the eggs and vanilla, then stir in the flour. Pour the batter into the prepared pan. Swirl the mint pesto into the batter.

Bake for about 25 minutes, or until the brownies begin to pull away from the sides of the pan. For best results, allow to cool completely before cutting.

Makes 16 to 24 brownies, depending on how you cut them

Congo Bars

Here's a one-bowl wonder for the next time you want to make an irresistible treat that will please grownups and children alike. These may seem slightly underbaked when it is time to remove them from the oven, especially if you break the rules and cut them while still hot, but that's because they are so moist. Use the visual clues of a browned top and edges that are just beginning to pull away from the sides of the pan, to determine when they are done.

---

10 Tablespoons (1¼ sticks) unsalted butter, melted
2 cups packed brown sugar
3 large eggs
1½ cups whole wheat pastry flour
1 cup all-purpose flour
2½ teaspoons baking powder
½ teaspoon salt
1 teaspoon ground cinnamon
1 cup unsweetened shredded coconut
¾ cup dark chocolate chips
½ cup white chocolate chips
½ cup chopped macadamia nuts
¼ cup cacao nibs, optional but delicious

Preheat the oven to 350 degrees. Butter a 9x13-inch baking dish, or coat it with non-stick spray.

Combine the melted butter and brown sugar in a large mixing bowl. Stir in the eggs one at a time. Add the flours, baking powder, salt and cinnamon; mix well. Work in the coconut, dark and white chocolate chips, nuts and cacao nibs, if using. The batter will be stiff.

Transfer the batter to the prepared baking dish, smoothing it into an even layer. Bake for 25 to 30 minutes, or until the edges begin to pull away from the sides of pan and the center is almost firm. We want them a little underbaked. Cool completely on a wire rack. Cut into bars by making 8 long cuts and 3 short cuts across for 24 pieces or 6 long and 5 short cuts across for 30.

Makes 24 to 30 bars

My Best Pumpkin Pie

Thanksgiving dinner isn't complete at our house until we've had this pie. One year I made it the night before and my husband and I had eaten half of it by the time we went to bed. You may think the graham cracker crust is odd, but that's what most people say makes it so delicious. You may have more filling than the crust will hold. Pour the extra into a small baking dish and bake it with the pie for a cook's treat.

---

1 cup sugar
1 teaspoon ground cinnamon
¼ teaspoon freshly grated nutmeg
¼ teaspoon ground cloves
⅛ teaspoon salt
2 large eggs
1 can (15 ounces) pumpkin (not pie filling)
1 cup heavy cream
1 prepared 9-inch graham cracker pie shell
Whipped cream or vanilla ice cream, for serving, if desired

Preheat the oven to 425 degrees.

Combine the sugar with the cinnamon, nutmeg, cloves and salt. Add the eggs and beat at medium speed with an electric mixer for 2 to 3 minutes or until fluffy. With the mixer at low speed, blend in the pumpkin, and then the cream.

Place the pie shell on a baking sheet. Pour the pumpkin mixture into the pie shell. Carefully place the baking sheet in the center of the oven. Bake for 20 minutes, and then reduce the heat to 375 degrees. Continue baking for about 35 minutes, or until a knife inserted into the center comes out clean.

Cool on a wire rack. Serve slightly warm, if desired, with whipped cream or ice cream. Refrigerate any leftovers.

Makes 8 servings

Sesame Seed Ice Cream

Dig out that ice cream machine, you'll need it here. This rich ice cream cries out for a hint of chocolate so you might try garnishing with a mixture of chopped chocolate and sesame seeds or serve it layered into a parfait with chocolate cake crumbs.

---

1 pint (2 cups) heavy cream
1 pint (2 cups) half-and-half
1 cup toasted tahini
½ cup sugar
1 teaspoon vanilla extract
Dash salt

Combine all of the ingredients using a blender or hand-held immersion mixer.

Freeze according to your ice cream machine's manufacturer instructions.

Makes 1 quart

Spicy Pumpkin Squares

I've been making this dessert for years. It seems somewhat wholesome to me with the whole grains and pumpkin. Part cheesecake, part pumpkin pie and part crumbly topping, these rich little nuggets are hard to resist.

¼ cup whole wheat flour
¾ cup rolled oats
¼ cup packed brown sugar
4 Tablespoons (½ stick) unsalted butter, chilled
½ cup finely chopped walnuts
1 package (8 ounces) cream cheese, softened
½ cup sugar
¾ cup pumpkin puree
2 large eggs
1 teaspoon ground allspice
1 teaspoon vanilla extract
⅛ teaspoon freshly grated nutmeg

Preheat the oven to 350 degrees. Lightly butter an 8-inch square baking pan, or coat it with non-stick spray.

Combine the flour, oats and brown sugar in a medium bowl. Using a pastry blender, cut in the butter until the mixture resembles fine crumbs. Stir in the nuts. Set aside ¾ cup for the topping. Press the remaining mixture into the bottom of the prepared pan (the flat side of a small measuring cup works well for this). Bake for 10 minutes. Cool on a wire rack for 10 minutes.

Meanwhile, using an electric mixer, beat the cream cheese and sugar until fluffy. Beat in the pumpkin, then the eggs, allspice, vanilla and nutmeg. Blend until smooth. Spread the cream cheese mixture evenly over the baked crust. Sprinkle with the reserved topping, pressing down lightly. Bake for an additional 30 minutes, or until the top just begins to brown.

Cool completely before cutting into 25 1½-inch squares. Best served chilled.

Makes 25

Fresh Fruit and Lavender Parfaits

The only thing you can do to make fresh blueberries and peaches taste better is to add lavender whipped cream. Other berries would work as well, on their own or with the peaches. Use well-chilled fruits for a refreshing summer dessert. For best results, look for whipping cream that is not ultra-pasteurized.

---

1 cup whipping cream, chilled
3 Tablespoons Lavender Sugar (see below)
1 cup crumbled crisp coconut macaroon cookies (or amaretti)
2 cups blueberries or chunks of peaches (or nectarines), or a combination
1 teaspoon dried lavender buds, for garnish

Combine the whipping cream with the lavender sugar in a medium mixing bowl. Whip at high speed until the cream has doubled in volume and will hold a soft peak.

In four parfait or wine glasses, alternate layers of the cookies, the fruit and the whipped cream twice. Sprinkle each dessert with ¼ teaspoon of the lavender buds. Serve immediately.

Makes 4 servings

Lavender Sugar: Grind 1 cup granulated sugar with 2 Tablespoons dried lavender buds in a blender until the sugar takes on a purple hue and the lavender buds are no longer visible. Use extra for sweetening lemonade or tea or for baked goods.

Blueberry Oat Pie

I so wanted this recipe to produce bars that you could pick up and eat out of hand. After numerous attempts, I had to abandon that idea. This flavor combination is sensational, however, so I offer you a pie-shaped dessert to make at the height of blueberry season.

1½ cups rolled oats
½ cup whole wheat pastry flour
½ cup packed brown sugar
½ cup chopped hazelnuts
1 teaspoon ground cinnamon
¼ teaspoon freshly grated nutmeg
2 dashes salt
½ cup (1 stick) unsalted butter, melted
2 cups fresh blueberries
¼ cup turbinado sugar
1 Tablespoon vanilla extract
Vanilla ice cream, for serving

Preheat the oven to 350 degrees. Coat an 8-inch pie tin with non-stick spray.

In a medium mixing bowl combine the oats, flour, brown sugar, hazelnuts, cinnamon, nutmeg and salt. Add the melted butter and stir well, until all the dry ingredients are moist. Set aside 1 cup of this for a topping. Evenly press the remaining oatmeal mixture into the bottom of the prepared pan (use the flat side of a small measuring cup for this). Bake the crust for 10 minutes; remove from oven and cool for 10 minutes more. Keep the oven on.

Toss the blueberries with the turbinado sugar and vanilla.

SAVORY ASIDE

Zest a peel.

Citrus zest can be a valuable component to a recipe. Plenty of options exist to help you remove just the colored part of the peel. Two of my favorites are a zesting tool and the Microplane zester. The zesting tool is a row of small holes fashioned onto a handle that is easy to hold. The Microplane zester, a knockoff from the woodworker's toolbox, makes quick work of grating nutmeg, chocolate and ginger as well. If you don't have a special tool, use your potato peeler to shave off the zest and then mince it with a knife.

After the crust has cooled for 10 minutes, spread the blueberries in an even layer over it. Top the blueberries with an even layer of the remaining oatmeal mixture, pressing down gently.

Bake for 15 minutes. Turn pan around and bake 15 to 20 minutes more, or until the berries are bubbling and the top is beginning to brown.

Cut into 8 wedges. Serve warm with ice cream.

Makes 8 servings

Cacao Nib-Orange Crepes

At first glance, this combination of ricotta crepes and fresh oranges may look like a complicated recipe, but it really isn't. Just take it one step at a time. You will be amazed by what a light, not so sweet, dessert it is. Making crepes is a wonderful skill to master since you can use them to prepare so many different dishes, sweet or savory. See page 168 for information about cutting the oranges into supremes. This dish would not be out of place at your next festive brunch.

For the crepes:
2/3 cup milk
2/3 cup water
3 large eggs
3 Tablespoons unsalted butter, melted and cooled slightly
1 cup Wondra flour, or other instant flour
3 Tablespoons cacao nibs, ground, plus 1 Tablespoon left whole, for garnish
1/4 teaspoon salt

For the filling:
2 cups whole milk ricotta cheese
Zest from 1 large orange, about 1 Tablespoon
3 Tablespoons honey
1/8 teaspoon salt

For the garnish:
1 Tablespoon unsalted butter
2 teaspoons honey
2 large oranges, cut into supremes

Place the crepe ingredients into the blender in the order given. Whirl until well mixed. Allow to rest in the refrigerator for at least 15 minutes.

To cook the crepes, place a crepe pan (or a 9-inch non-stick skillet) over medium-high heat. When the pan is hot enough for water to sizzle when dropped on the surface, pour in 1/4 cup of the batter and swirl the pan to cover the bottom. Cook for a minute or so, until the top is nearly dry. Carefully turn to cook the other side for about 30 seconds. Transfer to a plate and continue cooking the remaining batter. (*Crepes can be prepared ahead of serving time. Wrap well and refrigerate for up to two days or freeze. Bring to room temperature before assembling this dessert.*)

To prepare the filling, mix the ricotta cheese with the orange zest, honey and salt. (*Make this a day or two before serving, if desired, and bring to room temperature before assembling this dessert.*)

Just before serving, thinking of the crepe as a clock, place ¼ cup of the ricotta filling between 3:00 and 6:00 on each of 8 crepes. Fold the crepes in half and then in half again. Transfer the crepes to four dessert plates, arranging two of them so the points overlap slightly.

To prepare the garnish: Melt the butter in a 9-inch sauté pan over medium-high heat. Stir in the honey. Drain the orange segments and add to the pan; swirl the pan to coat these with the butter-honey mixture and heat briefly. Divide this topping evenly over the crepes. Garnish each with a sprinkling of the whole cacao nibs. Serve right away.

Makes 4 servings

Boston Cream Pie

My Mom often prepared this dessert from a box when I was a kid and it was always my favorite. I experimented with it for years, trying to make a good, moist version from scratch. The cake is key. I find that one called 'Rich and Tender Yellow Cake' from Cook's Illustrated.com is just right, however, you could always use a boxed mix with good results. Most cake recipes make two layers. Wrap the extra layer well and freeze it so you will be ready to make another one of these later. The addition of spices in the pastry cream elevates my childhood passion to a somewhat sophisticated grown-up indulgence.

---

1 9-inch layer made from your favorite yellow cake recipe
2 cups Spiced Pastry Cream, recipe follows
1¼ cups Chocolate Glaze, recipe follows

Using a large serrated knife, split the cake into two layers. Place the bottom layer onto a serving plate. Spread Spiced Pastry Cream evenly on the bottom layer; top with the other half of the cake, cut side down. Pour Chocolate Glaze over the top; use an offset spatula to spread it out evenly, as necessary (you may have some extra for a cook's treat). It looks nice if a bit of the glaze runs down the sides. Refrigerate until ready to serve, but bring to room temperature before serving.

Makes 8 servings

Spiced Pastry Cream

1¾ cups milk
2 teaspoons orange zest
Seeds from 8 green cardamom pods (½ teaspoon)
½ of a cinnamon stick
Pinch of freshly grated nutmeg
2 large egg yolks
⅓ cup sugar
2 Tablespoons cornstarch
⅛ teaspoon salt
1 teaspoon vanilla extract

Bring the milk to a rolling boil in a medium saucepan over medium heat. Remove from heat. Stir in the orange zest, cardamom, cinnamon stick and nutmeg; cover and steep for 30 minutes. Strain through a fine mesh strainer and set aside.

In a medium, heatproof bowl lightly beat the egg yolks and keep handy by the stovetop.

In another medium saucepan combine the sugar, cornstarch and salt. Place over medium heat and gradually add the spiced milk. Cook, stirring constantly, until it begins to thicken. Continue to cook and stir for 1 minute. Slowly, while stirring, pour half this mixture into the beaten egg yolks. Return the pan to heat, stir the egg/milk mixture back in. Cook, stirring, for 1 minute more or until the pastry cream will coat the back of a spoon. Remove from heat and stir in the vanilla. Transfer to a bowl and lay a sheet of plastic wrap over the surface of the pastry cream to prevent a skin from forming. Cool to room temperature.

Makes 2 cups

Chocolate Glaze

8 ounces bittersweet chocolate, chopped
1 cup heavy cream

Place the chocolate in a medium heatproof bowl. Bring the heavy cream to a rolling boil, watching carefully to prevent boiling over. Pour this over the chocolate in a bowl and let stand for 3 minutes without stirring. Then stir the cream into the chocolate (this looks like a disaster at first, just keep going). When the glaze is completely smooth, set aside until it is cool enough to top the cake without running off the sides, 2½ to 3 hours.

Makes 1⅓ cups

SAVORY ASIDE

Tea as an herb?

All types of tea—green, white, black and oolong--are produced from the *Camellia sinensis* plant. Since it is the leaves of the shrubby evergreen plant that are used, we can call it an herb. Brewed tea adds a savory, interesting flavor to marinades for fish and puts a new twist on cooking rice or grains. Dried tea leaves also impart an unusual, yet pleasing, taste to baked goods.

Green Tea Cakes with White Chocolate-Lavender Ganache

I learned this unusual method for mixing a cake from *Cook's Illustrated*. The result is a lovely tender cake and, with the addition of matcha, it's a fabulous green color with a pronounced green tea flavor. Look for brilliant green matcha powder (ground tea leaves) any place that sells loose tea. Initially I wanted to make this into little petite-fours with the ganache as a glaze. You could certainly do that by baking the batter in a 9x13-inch pan, then cutting squares or rectangles. That's a good deal more work than making simple cupcakes, but the presentation is well worth the effort, in my opinion.

---

1 cup hot tap water
1 Tablespoon matcha (green tea powder)
6 large egg whites (¾ cup)
1 teaspoon vanilla extract
2¼ cups cake flour
1¾ cups sugar
3 Tablespoons buttermilk powder
4 teaspoons baking powder
1 teaspoon salt
12 Tablespoons (1½ sticks) unsalted butter, softened
1 batch White Chocolate-Lavender Ganache, whipped (recipe follows)
2 Tablespoons lavender buds, or 24 candied flowers, for garnish, if desired

Preheat the oven to 350 degrees. Line two 12-cup muffin tins with paper cupcake liners. (If you only have one muffin tin, that's fine, you can bake the cupcakes in two batches. Just let the pan cool between batches.)

Pour the hot water into a 2-cup measure and whisk in the matcha. To this, add the egg whites and vanilla; whisk well. Set aside.

Combine the cake flour, sugar, buttermilk powder, baking powder and salt in the bowl of a stand mixer fitted with the paddle attachment (or use an electric mixer). Cut the butter into 6 pieces and add to the bowl, beating at low speed until the mixture takes on a somewhat coarse, sandy appearance and holds together when pressed between your fingers.

Mix in all but ½ cup of the egg/tea mixture and beat on medium speed for 1½ minutes. Scrape down the sides and bottom of the bowl with a rubber spatula. Add the remaining egg/tea mixture; beat 30 seconds more. Scrape the bowl and the paddle. Beat another 30 seconds.

Fill the cupcake liners two-thirds full. Bake for 10 minutes, turn the pan around. If baking with two muffin tins, rotate the pans on the racks. Bake for another 10 minutes or until the top springs back when lightly touched. Cool for 5 minutes on a rack. Remove cupcakes from the pan and cool completely on a wire rack.

To frost the cupcakes, use a pastry bag fitted with a large star tip to pipe the ganache in concentric circles, or simply use a knife to spread on a thick layer. Sprinkle the cakes with the lavender buds or top each with a candied flower.

Makes 24 cupcakes

White Chocolate-Lavender Ganache

Ganache is a versatile dessert component. Used before it cools, ganache can be poured over cakes as a glaze. After it has cooled, ganache can be whipped, as we do here, or even rolled into truffles. This creamy, dreamy version can be prepared in advance and frozen before whipping. Allow to cool completely before freezing. Thaw in refrigerator and then bring to room temperature before using.

1²/₃ cups heavy cream
5 teaspoons lavender buds, crushed
1 pound high-quality white chocolate, coarsely chopped

Combine the cream and lavender in a heavy 2-quart saucepan. Bring to a boil; boil and stir for one minute. Remove the pan from the heat; cover and let stand for 30 minutes.

Meanwhile, place the chopped chocolate into a deep, medium bowl. Have a dry fine-meshed sieve at the ready.

After 30 minutes, return the lavender cream to the heat. Bring to a boil again. Watching carefully so that it doesn't boil over, let the cream boil for 30 seconds. Then pour the lavender cream through the sieve into the bowl with the chocolate. Push on the sieved lavender with the back of a wooden spoon to squeeze out all the cream. Allow to stand, undisturbed for 3 minutes.

Then use a rubber spatula to stir the melting chocolate into the hot cream until the chocolate is completely incorporated and the mixture is smooth. Transfer to a shallow dish and allow to cool completely, at least 5 hours.

With an electric mixer, whip the cooled ganache at medium speed until it is light and fluffy, a minute or two depending on your machine.

Makes about 2½ cups ganache, 3½ when whipped

Spices used in Hot or Cold Chai, page 223

Spicy Extras: Condiments, sauces and basics

This final chapter is a collection of recipes to accent other recipes or punch up everyday cooking. Think of these spicy extras as accessories, jewelry for your food, if you will.

We use some unusual ingredients here. Nasturtiums, cheery little flowers that couldn't be easier to grow, give color and flavor to Kaleidoscope Butter. Using the spicy seed pods take this one step further.

Kaleidoscope Butter is a fanciful garnish to use for a splash of color on otherwise plain dishes like steamed veggies or a grilled chicken breast. Follow the same method of combining herbs and spices into softened butter to create other tasty compound butters. Keep a roll of one of these in the freezer for whenever you want a quick finish for a dish.

Pesto is another handy condiment to keep in the freezer. We offer four versions in this chapter, made from not only basil but also from arugula and mint. It is a good idea to freeze pesto in small portions, maybe just a tablespoon or two. Some folks like to use ice cube trays for portion control.

A variety of dishes in this book call for pesto, an example of its versatility. Don't overlook pesto as a sandwich spread, pizza topping or final flourish to soups.

I could say the same thing for roasted chiles. You've seen them come up time and again through-out these pages. Roasting chiles is easy to accomplish while providing a high-quality addition to your recipes.

Sofrito is brimming with chiles, too, but they aren't roasted. This savory concoction of onions, garlic, chiles and spices will likely find a spot in your repertoire once you give it a try.

This is also true of making your own mustard. It is easier than you may suspect and, after trying Beer-Thyme Mustard, you will be brimming with ideas for your own combos. The key with mustard is to leave it at room temperature for days or even weeks until it has mellowed to the level of heat you desire. It is always hottest just after mixing. Refrigeration will stop it from losing pungency.

While oils infused with garlic, herbs and spices should always be kept in the refrigerator and used within a week or so, flavored vinegars will last and last. Shiso in a Bottle gives you a basic recipe. I also love to make tarragon vinegar by following the same method.

Full credit for my knowledge of making flavored vinegars goes to Jerry Traunfeld's *Herbfarm Cookbook*. Until I read that book, I had been using far too little of any herb to create an intense infusion.

Flavored vinegars are a wonderful way to use up the bounty of fresh herbs as the growing season winds down, especially if you end up in the emergency situation of an impending first freeze. After a couple of weeks of waiting, you can bring those fresh summer flavors back, using the vinegar on salads and other winter dishes.

Shiso is a showy herb to grow. Plant it anywhere you might plant basil; they are similar in habit and needs. Shiso comes in purple or green varieties that make nice edging plants. Both varieties taste the same, a sort of cinnamon-basil or spicy-thyme, depending upon whom you ask.

Be sure to plant some parsley, too. The curly-leafed variety is a prettier garden specimen, but the flat-leafed type is better for use in the kitchen. Parsley is a biennial, meaning that it will grow foliage the first year and then produce flowers in its second season. If you let these flowers go to seed, you'll have a steady supply of parsley for as long as you want it.

Chefs have long used leaves of parsley as a garnish. Other herbs work, as well. Sprigs of thyme or tarragon can be dramatic while the cucumber taste of pretty borage flowers is surprising. It is fun to make your food look as good as it tastes.

Whether it's as a flavorful beginning of Turmeric Pasta or Green Sofrito or a final flourish of Thousand Island Dressing and Seeded Croutons, jump right in and add some bling to your cooking.

Enchilada Sauce

Chilly winter weather is the perfect time for hearty Mexican foods. This recipe is great for enchiladas, of course, but I like to serve it over my Crispy Chile Rellenos (page 122) as well. Like most enchilada sauces, this one is rather thin so don't be surprised. Try it as a base for Mexican pizza, too.

1½ cups chicken stock
½ cup tomato sauce
1 Tablespoon ground New Mexican chile
1 teaspoon vinegar
¾ teaspoon salt
¼ teaspoon Mexican oregano
¼ teaspoon ground cumin
⅛ teaspoon granulated garlic
1 Tablespoon olive oil
1 clove garlic, peeled and left whole
1 Tablespoon all-purpose flour

In a 2-cup measure or a small bowl, combine the first eight ingredients (chicken stock through granulated garlic). Set aside.

Heat the olive oil with the whole clove of garlic in a medium skillet over medium-high heat. When the oil is aromatic with the garlic, remove and discard the clove. Slowly add the flour to the oil; cook and stir for one minute. Continuing to stir, add the chicken stock mixture. Bring to a boil, reduce heat to medium and simmer hard for five minutes more.

Makes 2 cups

Thousand Island Dressing

I like to make my own salad dressings because the commercial varieties tend to the sweet side. This version of the classic makes a delicious sandwich spread and is a must for a grilled Rueben sandwich.

½ cup mayonnaise
¼ cup bottled chili (aka cocktail) sauce
2 Tablespoons finely chopped green olives
2 Tablespoons lemon juice
2 Tablespoons milk
3 teaspoons snipped chives
½ teaspoon sweet Spanish paprika
½ teaspoon salt
¼ teaspoon freshly milled black pepper

Place all ingredients in a jar with a lid and shake well.

Makes ¾ cup

Speckled Cheese Sauce

Who doesn't love cauliflower or broccoli with cheese sauce? What about macaroni and cheese? You'll be a hero. Stir a bit of salsa into this sauce and, presto, you've got chile con queso. It is easier to finely grate the cheese if it is cold.

---

2 Tablespoons unsalted butter
⅓ cup minced red bell pepper
2 Tablespoons minced green bell pepper
2 Tablespoons all-purpose flour
1 cup hot milk
¾ cup (1½ ounces) finely grated cheddar cheese
¾ cup (1½ ounces) finely grated Fontina
¼ teaspoon salt
Dash cayenne pepper, or to taste

Melt the butter in a heavy saucepan over medium high heat. Add the bell peppers; cook, stirring regularly, about 3 minutes. Sprinkle the flour over the butter and bell peppers; mix in well. Continue cooking and stirring 3 minutes more until mixture is thick and just beginning to brown. Slowly pour in the hot milk. Bring to a boil, stirring constantly to prevent scorching, until the sauce is thick and bubbly, another 3 minutes or so. Remove from heat and add the cheeses slowly, stirring well after each addition. Season with the salt and cayenne, adjusting as necessary to taste.

Makes about 1½ cups

Annatto Oil

Whole annatto seeds remind me of fish bowl gravel but taste lots better. This deeply colored oil has a tendency to leave temporary stains on counters or clothing. They will fade but use caution if you're concerned. Annatto Oil is called for in A Golden Chicken (page 108). You might also try it for a Latin-flavored vinaigrette or use it for roasting potatoes.

½ cup olive oil
2 Tablespoons annatto seeds

Combine the olive oil and annatto seeds in a small saucepan. Heat over medium-high heat for 3 to 5 minutes, until the oil takes on a deep golden color. (Watch for spattering as the oil heats.)

Remove from heat and allow to cool. Strain and use as desired. Store extras in the refrigerator for no more than 1 week.

Makes ½ cup

SAVORY ASIDE

Herb oil warning.

We've discussed it time and again at the website: herbed oils should be stored in the refrigerator for no more than one week. Everyone seems to have a "what if…" question, but the food safety experts remain firm on every scenario. The vegetables and herbs we use to make flavored oils harbor moisture that can produce botulism, a potentially fatal food poisoning. Definitely not something you want to play with. For safety's sake, make herb oils in small batches and use them right away.

Basil Pesto

Refreshing and sparkling with flavor, here's a basic pesto recipe that will serve you well. One half cup basil may not seem like enough; just be sure your measuring cup is really crammed full. Pine nuts are a traditional ingredient. To toast them, shake in a small, dry skillet over medium-high heat until they begin to get light brown spots. Cool completely before using.

½ cup (packed) fresh basil leaves
½ cup toasted pine nuts
½ cup (packed) fresh parsley leaves
¼ cup freshly grated Parmesan cheese
2 cloves garlic, quartered
2 Tablespoons extra virgin olive oil
Freshly milled black pepper, to taste
Kosher salt, to taste

In the work bowl of a food processor fitted with the steel blade, combine the basil, pine nuts, parsley, Parmesan cheese, garlic and olive oil. Process to a fine paste. Taste; adjust seasonings as desired.

Transfer to a glass container and refrigerate. This pesto will keep for weeks in the refrigerator, although the top will harmlessly discolor. A thin coat of olive oil will prevent this.

Makes about 1 cup

Spinach Pesto

I love this pesto for the fresh, fresh flavors. Another advantage is that it can be made in the dead of winter when basil is long gone.

---

2 cups (packed) fresh spinach leaves, well-washed and stemmed
½ cup (packed) fresh parsley, preferably Italian flat leaf
½ cup chopped walnuts, toasted
¼ cup freshly grated Parmesan cheese
3 cloves garlic, peeled and quartered
3 Tablespoons extra virgin olive oil
¼ teaspoon salt
⅛ teaspoon freshly milled black pepper

Place all ingredients into the workbowl of a food processor fitted with the steel blade. Process to a fine paste, scraping down the sides of the bowl 2 or 3 times. Taste; adjust seasonings as necessary.

Transfer to a glass container and refrigerate. This pesto will keep for weeks in the refrigerator. The top will harmlessly discolor, although a thin coat of olive oil can prevent this.

Makes about 1 cup

Cooking School Pesto

This is my favorite pesto, one that I use all the time. I love the combination of basil and almonds plus the pretty little flecks of red from the tomatoes. These are the ingredients we used at Casa Caponetti cooking classes in Italy. Laura Caponetti didn't use specific measurements; this is what works in my American kitchen.

---

1 cup (packed) fresh basil leaves (about ¾ ounce)
1 small clove garlic, peeled and quartered
¼ cup olive oil
¼ cup pine nuts
¼ cup sliced almonds
4 small cherry tomatoes
A few pinches of kosher salt
⅓ cup (packed) Parmesan cheese

Place all ingredients into the workbowl of a food processor fitted with the steel blade. Process to a fine paste, scraping down the sides of the bowl 2 or 3 times. Taste; adjust seasonings as necessary.

Transfer to a glass container and refrigerate. This pesto will keep for weeks in the refrigerator. The top will harmlessly discolor, although a thin coat of olive oil can prevent this.

Makes about ¾ cup

Mint Pesto

This distinctive dessert pesto is terrific with chocolate. Try it as a filling for sandwich cookies or mix some into chocolate sauce for ice cream or cake. The Mint Pesto Brownies on page 188 have won rave reviews in the test kitchen and beyond. I like to make this with peppermint; however, spearmint is a fine option as well.

½ cup macadamia nuts
2 cups packed fresh mint leaves
⅓ cup honey
1 Tablespoon vanilla extract

In a food processor fitted with the steel blade, briefly chop the nuts before adding the remaining ingredients. Puree until reduced to a paste.

If you're not using this right away, transfer it to a glass container, lay plastic wrap over the top so it is touching the pesto, keeping air from penetrating the pesto. Store in the refrigerator for up to a month.

Makes about 1 cup

Beer-Thyme Mustard

The Making Mustard at Home article is one of my website's most popular. You might be surprised how easy it is to mix up a batch. This recipe gives you a jumping off point for creating your own flavors. Substitute wine for the beer (or use just plain water), change the herbs or try a different type of vinegar. As long as the proportions stay the same, you should have good results. We use dried onion and thyme here so as not to worry about refrigerating perishable ingredients.

¼ cup brown mustard seeds
¼ cup yellow mustard seeds
¾ cup flat amber beer (or beer of your choice)
1 Tablespoon mustard powder
1 Tablespoon dried minced onion
2 teaspoons dried thyme leaves
½ cup cider vinegar
1 teaspoon salt

Soak the mustard seeds in the beer overnight.

About 20 minutes before you are ready to make the mustard, stir the mustard powder, minced onion and thyme into the soaked seed mixture and allow to stand.

Place the mustard mixture in a blender with the vinegar and salt. Grind until it reaches the consistency of a paste, with some seeds remaining visible. Transfer to a glass jar, cover and let stand 4 to 5 days before using. Store in refrigerator.

Makes about 1¼ cups

Dad's Pickled Garlic

My dad always had a big jar of pickled garlic in the refrigerator. He loved it and swore that eating this garlic everyday kept the mosquitoes away. My mom said the biting bugs chose her just because she was sweeter. Who knows which is true? Sometimes he cheated on his own recipe and just pickled the garlic in the liquid left from jars of peperoncini.

---

2 Tablespoons white vinegar
3 Tablespoons water
1 teaspoon sugar
½ teaspoon pickling spices
2 bulbs of garlic, separated into unpeeled cloves

Combine the vinegar, water, sugar and pickling spices in a small saucepan. Bring to a boil over medium heat. Set aside to cool.

In another small pan, cover the garlic cloves with water and bring to a boil. Boil for about five minutes. Remove from heat and allow to cool. When garlic is cool enough to handle, peel each clove and place them in a clean half-pint jar. Pour vinegar mixture over the garlic in jar. Refrigerate for at least a week before eating.

Makes about 1 pint

Kaleidoscope Butter

With their snappy radish-like flavor and colorful, edible flowers, nasturtiums provide an abundance of opportunity for the creative cook. Combine the leaves with other greens in salads or tuck them into sandwiches. The round shape of the leaves also makes an attractive base for appetizers or other small treats. Chopped or shredded, they can be used to replace the traditional parsley garnish called for in so many recipes.

½ cup (1 stick) unsalted butter, softened to room temperature
2 Tablespoons minced fresh nasturtium flowers (use different colors, if possible)
1 Tablespoon minced fresh nasturtium leaves
1 Tablespoon minced nasturtium seedpods
Salt and freshly milled black pepper, to taste

Mix the minced flowers, leaves and seedpods into the softened butter. Taste for salt and pepper; add in small increments as desired.

Spread the butter mixture into a long strip down the center of a 10-inch length of waxed paper, stopping about 3 inches from the edge on each side. Fold the paper over lengthwise so the butter is in the center and gently push in and under to form it into a smooth log (a bench scraper or ruler will make this process much more efficient). Continue rolling the wrapped butter log into a cylinder; twist the ends shut and chill.

To serve, cut slices from the log and place atop hot, cooked meat or vegetables.

To store, wrap again in foil or plastic. Keep for one week in the refrigerator or freeze for up to three months.

Makes ½ cup

Shiso in a Bottle

More method than recipe, condiments don't get much easier than this. Tart and tangy, yet slightly sweet, shiso vinegar is wonderful over green salads that include fruit. It takes on a gorgeous jewel-like hue if you use purple shiso.

Cram into a small glass jar with a tight-fitting lid as many shiso leaves as you can. Pour in as much champagne vinegar as the jar will hold. Fasten on the lid and allow to stand at room temperature for at least 3 weeks, as long as 6.

Strain the flavored vinegar to remove the shiso leaves. Store at room temperature in a bottle with a tight-fitting lid. Use the flavored vinegar in salad dressings, sauces or when marinating meats and fish.

Turmeric Pasta

Making your own pasta is a worthwhile endeavor, not only for the sense of accomplishment but also because it is so doggone good. Semolina, a traditional ingredient in pasta, is wheat flour that is more coarsely ground than other flours. I often find it at the supermarket among the other grains. The hint of turmeric here gives a slight peppery-ginger flavor and a sexy color to the dough.

---

1 cup semolina
1 cup all-purpose flour
¾ teaspoon turmeric
⅛ teaspoon salt
½ cup warm water, plus more as needed

Toss the dry ingredients together in a medium mixing bowl. Stir in the ½ cup water. When the mixture is too stiff to stir with a spoon, begin kneading in more water, 1 Tablespoon at a time, to form a firm but pliable dough.

If rolling the dough out by hand, continue kneading a few minutes more. Wrap in plastic and let rest 30 minutes. Divide into four or more portions and roll to desired thickness with a rolling pin. Keep the dough covered when not working with it.

If rolling the dough through a machine or hand-cranked roller, wrap in plastic and let rest 30 minutes. Divide the dough into four or more portions; keep them covered when you are not working them. Feed each portion into the machine, set on the largest number, several times, folding the dough into thirds after each time through. Proceed with rolling into desired pasta form.

Makes 4 to 6 servings

SAVORY ASIDE

Noodles, ravioli or spaghetti.

Homemade pasta is an easy, yet impressive feat that offers flavorful rewards. It all starts with "sfolgia," the Italian word for an uncut sheet of pasta. How the sheet is cut determines the noodle. Lasagna noodles are a wide cut, fettuccini is thinner. When we sandwich a filling into the lasagna noodles, we get ravioli or even tortellini. Many pasta rollers come with attachments for extruding spaghetti or macaroni.

Roasted Chiles

You can buy jars of roasted peppers and chiles at the supermarket, but the taste is so much better if you do it yourself. Freshly roasted, they are much more firm and flavorful. You can do this with any fresh chile or bell pepper. I always just tear the bag open and use that to collect all the seeds and skin for easy clean-up.

Place whole peppers on a baking sheet under a broiler unit. Allow the skin to blacken and blister, turning often so that the entire surface appears this way. Remove from the broiler and place the pepper in a paper bag, folding the top over several times. Let stand for 5 minutes to steam. Remove from the bag and, without burning yourself, peel off the blackened skin. Slit down one side to open, remove seeds and stem.

Use right away or store submerged in oil in the refrigerator for no longer than 5 days.

Red Sofrito

Sofrito is the first step in preparing a Spanish paella, as well as a wide variety of Latin dishes. It is a delicious marinade for pork, to be served with rice and beans where sofrito is also a base. Think of it as a marinade for shrimp and chicken, too. Try frying parboiled potatoes in sofrito and then scramble a couple of eggs on the side for a hearty breakfast. Other ideas, like mixing it into sour cream for a baked potato topper and adding sofrito to softened butter for a colorful garnish on vegetables or meats and fish, should fuel your imagination. If you prefer a green sofrito, simply omit the last step of adding the tomato paste.

---

1 medium yellow onion, peeled
2 large cloves garlic, peeled
1 sweet yellow pepper, stemmed and seeded (aka: frying pepper, banana pepper)
1 Anaheim chile pepper, stemmed and seeded
1 small mild red chile, stemmed and seeded
1 jalapeno, stemmed and seeded
¼ cup packed fresh oregano leaves
¼ cup Annatto Oil (page 211)
½ teaspoon salt
2 Tablespoons tomato paste

Coarsely chop the onion, garlic, peppers and chiles; transfer to the bowl a food processor, along with the oregano leaves. Use pulses to chop further until the mixture is minced but not pureed. Set aside.

Heat the annatto oil in a large skillet set over medium heat; mix in the minced vegetables. This might make you cry, use the exhaust fan and avoid breathing in the steam. Stir frequently to cook the vegetables without browning until tender, about 10 minutes. (The vegetables will release a good bit of liquid at first so you won't need to stir as much, but watch closely as this liquid evaporates.) Remove the skillet from the heat but leave the stove on. Stir in the salt and tomato paste, working the paste into the vegetables with the back of a wooden spoon. Return the skillet to the heat; stir and fry for 2 to 3 minutes more.

Makes about ¾ cup

Hot or Cold Chai

These same spices make a delightful flavored coffee although you might want to double the amount for a full pot. Simply add the spices to the ground coffee before brewing. Beware, however, the next few pots of coffee may have a hint of spice.

---

1 cardamom pod, broken
¼ teaspoon dried orange peel
⅛ teaspoon freshly grated nutmeg
2 cups water
3 teaspoons tea leaves
½ cup milk
2 teaspoons turbinado sugar, or more to taste

Combine the cardamom, orange peel and nutmeg with the water in a saucepan. Bring to a boil; reduce heat and simmer, covered, for five minutes. Stir in the tea leaves, simmer another minute. Stir in milk; simmer, uncovered, for five minutes more. Strain through a fine mesh strainer or several layers of cheesecloth. Stir in sugar and serve. For an even spicier flavor, allow to cool then chill thoroughly and serve cold.

Makes about 2½ cups

SAVORY ASIDE

An Aromatic Stocking Stuffer.

Many folks enjoy the flavors of chai. Make a tasty little gift by combining the spices with tea leaves. Pack the mixture into a square of plastic wrap, pull up the corners to make a bundle then wrap again in tissue paper. Secure the little bundle with a ribbon and pop that into an attractive coffee cup. Easier yet, fill a metal tea ball with the spiced tea.

Seeded Croutons

Homemade croutons are far superior to store bought. You'll want to use "day-old" bread that is soft enough to absorb the olive oil but firm enough to cut into cubes. I sometimes leave half of a baguette in the bag it came in overnight, giving me the perfect texture, a little bit dried out for croutons.

½ teaspoon kosher salt
½ teaspoon white sesame seeds
½ teaspoon black sesame seeds
¼ teaspoon dill seeds
¼ teaspoon caraway seeds
⅛ teaspoon celery seeds
⅛ teaspoon freshly milled black pepper
¼ cup olive oil
4 cups ½-inch bread cubes

Preheat the oven to 400 degrees.

Combine the salt with all of the seeds and the black pepper in a small bowl. Stir in the olive oil.

Place the bread cubes in a mixing bowl and drizzle the seasoned olive oil over them. Use your hands to toss the bread in the oil to coat well. Transfer to a baking sheet.

Toast the croutons in the oven for 12 to 15 minutes, or until nicely browned and crisp.

Makes about 2 cups

Mom's Cornbread

This is the quick bread of my childhood, revered with a bowl of pinto beans. It also served as the base for the stuffing in our Thanksgiving turkey and is delightful with honey, molasses or, especially, pumpkin butter. These days I usually make it with whole wheat pastry flour and buttermilk (plus ¼ teaspoon baking soda) but if I write the recipe that way, I can't call it Mom's.

¾ cup cornmeal
¼ cup all-purpose flour
2 teaspoons baking powder
1 teaspoon salt
1 egg
1 Tablespoon vegetable oil
½ cup milk

Preheat the oven to 425 degrees. Coat an 8-inch pie pan with non-stick cooking spray.

Combine the cornmeal, flour, baking powder and salt on a sheet of waxed paper. Set aside.

In a small mixing bowl, beat the egg. Stir in the oil and milk. Add the dry ingredients; mixing just until moistened. Pour into the prepared pan and smooth the top.

Bake for 12 to 15 minutes, or until the top is lightly browned. Slice into wedges and serve right away.

Makes 4 to 6 servings

Resources

www.aPinchOf.com
You can find tons of information about individual herbs and spices, as well as herb gardening information and more recipes, at my website.

www.SproutPeople.org
This website is one-stop shopping for all your home sprouting needs. They offer kits and an amazing variety of high-quality seeds to sprout, plus helpful hints to get you started.

www.KingArthurFlour.com
I like King Arthur for its multitude of baking supplies. This is where I order my barley flakes, different yeasts and well-priced vanilla extract.

www.BobsRedMill.com
Bob's products are in most grocery stores and are my favorite source for corn flour, whole wheat pastry flour, assorted grains, unsweetened coconut and buttermilk powder. What you can't find at the supermarket, you'll find online. And if you are ever in the Portland, Oregon, area, you can stop by the big red mill for shopping and a tasty meal.

www.Amazon.com
This reliable workhorse of a website is the place to find some of the unusual items I like to use. Look here for papaya seed dressing and red sea salt, fennel pollen and cacao nibs.

www.sfherb.com
Buy in bulk and save with the San Francisco Herb Company. They have great variety and good quality ingredients that are delivered quickly.

www.Penderys.com
My favorite place for chiles and paprika, Pendery's has excellent products. Thanks to their informative catalog and website, you always know exactly what you are getting.

Index

Chervil
    about, 142
    in ham salad, 174
    peas and carrots, 144
Chicken
    cabbage and sausage supper, 107
    golden, 108
    pot pie, 109
    salad, 175
Chicken pot pie, 109
Chickpea flatbread, 68
Chickpea flour
    about, 68
    curry-garbanzo fish variation, 114
    flatbread, 68
    sesame wheat crackers, 69
Chile(s) *see also peppers*
    chipotle-jack dip, 8
    enchilada sauce, 208
    green, 42
    my best, 43
    relleno quiche, 89
    rellenos crispy, 122
    roasted, 221
Chile relleno quiche, 89
Chili powder
    about, 29
    in green chili, 42
    in spicy nut mix, 4
Chipotle-jack dip, 8
Chipotle mayonnaise, 111
Chives
    about, 164
    in asparagus ham roll-ups, 91
    in broccoli coins, 146
    in corn cakes, 18
    in egg and tuna roll-ups, 177
    in egg salad, 178
    in ricotta spread, 13
    in thousand island dressing, 209
    in vegetable tomato sauce, 139
Chocolate
    in congo bars, 189
    glaze, 200

    rosemary-lavender brownies, 187
    white, lavender ganache, 203
Chocolate glaze, 200
Chutney
    about, 129
    in curried millet, garbanzos, spinach, 129
Cinnamon
    about, 53, 60
    biscuits, 60
    in blueberry oat pie, 194
    in congo bars, 189
    in fruit crisp, 185
    in kasha, quinoa and couscous
        cereal, 77
    in pumpkin pie, 190
Cinnamon biscuits, 60
Citrus supreme, 168
Coconut
    in congo bars, 189
    in granola, 74
    in tropical fish, 113
Composed tuna salad, 179
Compound butter
    about, 206
    kaleidoscope, 218
Congo bars, 189
Cooking School Pesto, 214
Coriander
    about, 29
    in chili, 43
    in corn and black bean salad, 166
    in falafel, 133
Corn
    black bean salad and, 166
    cakes, 18
    in vaquero stew, 40
Corn and black bean salad with tortilla
        strip croutons, 166
Cornbread
    mom's, 225
    pecan stuffing, 158
Corn cakes with two toppings, 18
Couscous, kasha and quinoa cereal, 77
Crawfish fettuccini, 116

Cream cheese
    in bacon and thyme stuffed tomatoes, 17
    in cheese ball, 14
    eggs scrambled with sprouts, tomatoes
        and, 81
    in pumpkin squares, 192
    in strawberry stuffed French toast, 78
Crepes, cacao-nib orange, 196
Crispy chile rellenos, 122
Croutons
    seeded, 224
    tortilla strip, 167
Cucumber raita, 135
Cumin
    in bean spinach stew, 126
    in black bean and tomato topping, 20
    in breakfast tacos, 87
    in chili, 43
    in chipotle-jack dip, 8
    in falafel, 133
    in hummus, 6
    in taco meat filling, 99
    in taco stuffed baked potatoes, 156
    in tortilla strip croutons, 167
    in vaquero stew, 40
Curried halibut in paper, 112
Curried millet bowl with spinach and
        garbanzos, 129
Curried squash soup, 39
Curried vegetables, 121
Curry powder, 120
Cutting pasta sheets, 220

Dad's pickled garlic, 217
Daniel's Easter eggs, 84
Daniel's Mongolian salsa, 86
Dill
    about, 94, 142
    in cabbage and chicken sausage supper, 107
    in cheese ball, 14
    in cucumber raita, 135
    in egg salad, 178
    in fennel ravioli, 123

    in kasha acorn squash, 132
    in pan-fried potatoes, 155
    in potato paprikash, 154
    in rye muffins, 58
Dips
    almond-red pepper, 7
    chipotle-jack, 8
    salsa, quick fresh, 9
    savory-white bean, 4
    seeded hummus, 6
Double bean spinach stew, 126

Egg and tuna roll-ups, 177
Egg salad with walnut oil, 178
Eggplant
    extra, 140
    parmesans, 23
Eggplant extra, 140
Egg(s)
    best breakfast yet, 83
    breakfast fajitas, 88
    breakfast tacos, 87
    chile relleno quiche, 89
    Daniel's Easter, 84
    fried rice, 131
    herb garden quiche, 91
    in papaya-shrimp salad, 180
    polenta stacks, 82
    salad with walnut oil, 178
    tuna wrap, 177
    winter quiche, 90
Eggs scrambled with sprouts, tomatoes and cream
        cheese, 81
Enchilada sauce, 208
Epazote
    about, 3, 164
    in corn and black bean salad, 166
    quesadilla with zucchini filling, 11

Fajitas, 97
Falafel, 133
Fennel
    bulb, sliced and braised, 148

almonds in fruit crisp, 185
almonds and snow peas with lemon balm, 145
cheese puffs, 12
granola, 74
hazelnuts in blueberry oat pie, 194
macadamia in congo bars, 189
macadamia in mint pesto, 215
pecans in cardamom scones, 62
pecans in cornbread stuffing, 158
pecans in waffles, 80
spicy mixed, 4
walnuts in arugula orange salad, 169
walnuts in pumpkin squares, 192
walnuts in cheese ball, 14
walnuts in pasta with pesto, 24
Nutty cheese puffs, 12
Nutty granola, 74

Oatmeal
blueberry pie, 194
in fruit crisp, 185
in granola, 74
in pumpkin squares, 192
Old-Fashioned Ham Salad, 174
Onion(s)
granulated, in beef jerky, 100
soup, 38
in split pea stew, 44
tarts, 21
Onion salt
making, 152
in savory sweets, 153
Onion Tarts, 21
Orange(s)
arugula salad, 169
crepes, cacao nibs and, 196
cutting supremes, 168
zest in pastry cream, 199
zesting, 194
Oregano
about, 2
in chili, 43
in eggplant extra, 140
in eggplant parmesans, 23

in green chili, 42
Mexican, 42
in minestrone, 47
in ricotta spread, 13
in sofrito, 222
in vegetable tomato sauce, 139
in yellow squash sauté, 152
Oven baked falafel, 133

Papaya-shrimp salad, 180
Paprika
about, 3
in cauliflower gratin, 150
in cheese ball, 14
in Hungarian goulash, 49
in potato paprikash, 154
in thousand island dressing, 209
Parsley
about, 207
in basil pesto, 212
in chicken pot pie, 109
in chili, 43
in falafel, 133
in fried potatoes, 155
in meatballs, 103
in ricotta spread, 13
in white bean puree, 4
Pasta with spinach pesto, 24
Pasta, sunny side dish, 157
Pasta, turmeric, 220
Pastry cream, spiced, 199
Peaches
fruit and lavender parfaits, 193
fruit 'n barley flakes, 76
gingered, 75
Pecan-cornbread stuffing, 158
Pepper(s), *see also chiles*
Anaheim
in crispy chile rellenos, 122
in Spanish rice, 160
bell
in breakfast fajitas, 88
in calzones, 101
in cheese sauce, 210

9123002R0

Made in the USA
Charleston, SC
12 August 2011